THE PASSIONATE QUILTER

THE PASSIONATE QUILTER

MICHELE WALKER

PHOTOGRAPHY BY
SANDRA LOUSADA

EBURY PRESS LONDON

This book is dedicated to my mother
and to my father who very sadly did not live to see it published.

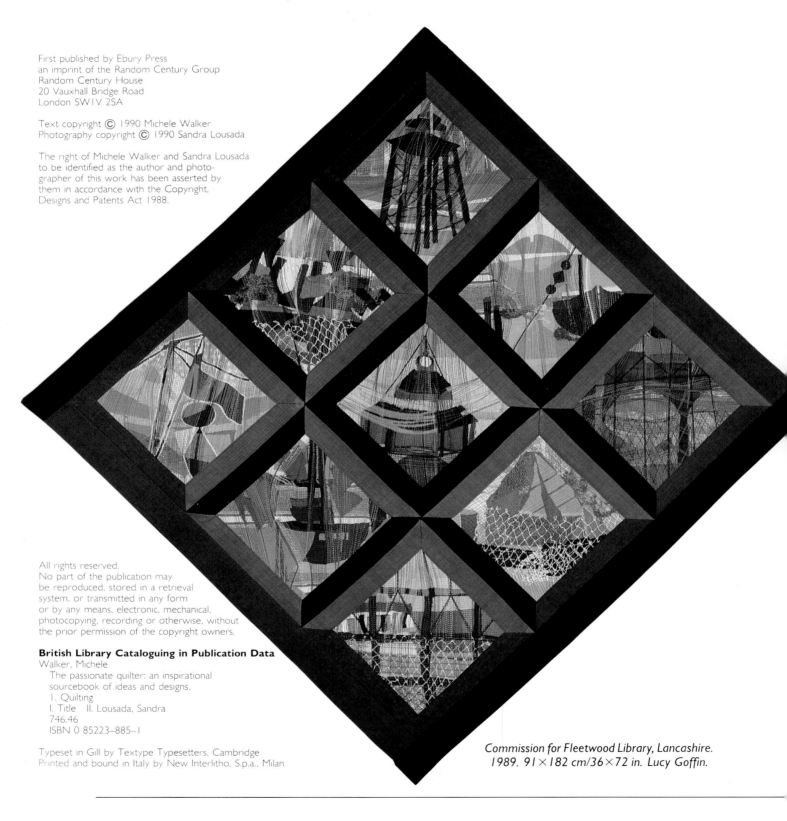

First published by Ebury Press
an imprint of the Random Century Group
Random Century House
20 Vauxhall Bridge Road
London SW1V 2SA

Text copyright © 1990 Michele Walker
Photography copyright © 1990 Sandra Lousada

The right of Michele Walker and Sandra Lousada
to be identified as the author and photographer of this work has been asserted by
them in accordance with the Copyright,
Designs and Patents Act 1988.

British Library Cataloguing in Publication Data
Walker, Michele
    The passionate quilter: an inspirational
    sourcebook of ideas and designs.
    1. Quilting
    I. Title   II. Lousada, Sandra
    746.46
    ISBN 0 85223–885–1

Typeset in Gill by Textype Typesetters, Cambridge
Printed and bound in Italy by New Interlitho, S.p.a., Milan

*Commission for Fleetwood Library, Lancashire.
1989. 91 × 182 cm/36 × 72 in. Lucy Goffin.*

CONTENTS
Introduction **6**

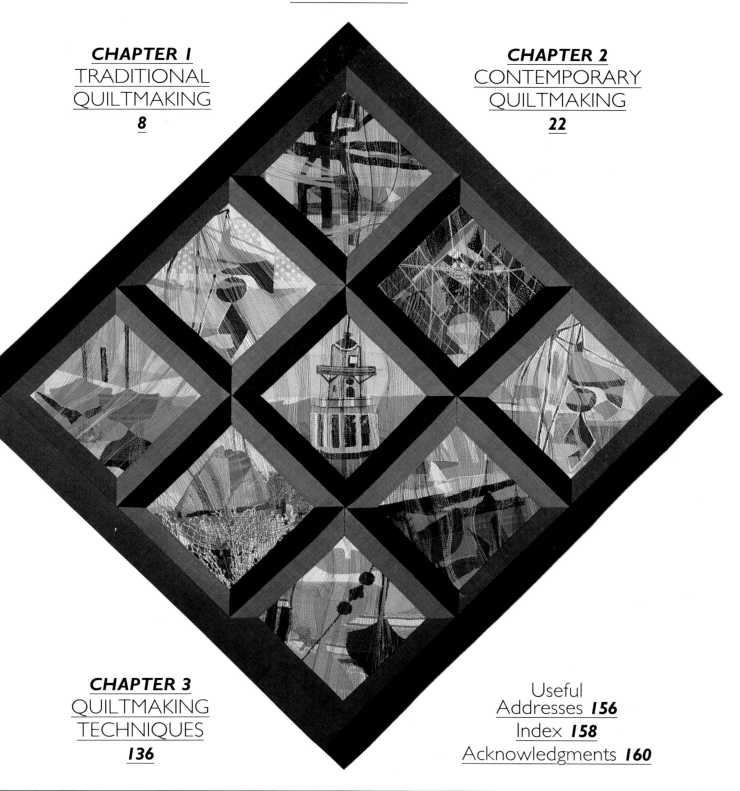

INTRODUCTION

This book celebrates the work of both traditional and contemporary quiltmakers. Quilts are not produced in isolation but are intrinsically part of the maker's life, which arouses curiosity in anyone interested in the subject. This book focuses on the creativity and motivation of the artists. Not all consider themselves either quiltmakers or quilters as the title suggests, but both the traditional and contemporary artists are united by the fact that they have chosen fabric and stitching as their preferred medium and have been influenced by the traditional quilt in the work they produce.

Today quiltmaking is no longer regarded as necessarily making a functional item. It is a language adopted by artists to express an idea or belief and to challenge and redefine the preconceptions of the tradition. For several decades traditional values – as in other disciplines, ceramics and jewellery, for example – have been turned upside down. Ceramics has crossed the boundary into sculpture and is now also viewed in a fine-art context. Jewellery is not just associated with precious metals; wood, plastic and paper are today considered viable materials.

The contemporary maker is not as accepting as in the past and requires a more challenging approach with greater emphasis on creativity. This has been partly the result of art-school graduates entering the craft and introducing influences from their particular area of study. For example, Jo Budd, who studied painting, combines the attitude of a fine artist with that of a craftsperson when she describes the fact that it is the content of the work that is of major importance, but adds that it must be made with a sensitivity for the medium being used.

Quiltmaking, which embraces patchwork, appliqué and quilting, offers so much for individual interpretation. The first steps may be quite tentative and you could begin by taking a traditional pattern, for example the 'Maple Leaf' block on page 140, and interpreting it for yourself with your own choice of fabrics and colours. This will familiarize you with the techniques and enable you to see the opportunities for adding to the tradition rather than just repeating it. Unfortunately a perfect copy will never capture the spontaneity of the original and is a poor legacy for succeeding quiltmakers.

The book is divided into three chapters. The first is about traditional quilts and women whom I regard as part of the last generation to work in this style. Until recently they were relatively unknown. One quilter described earning a living from quiltmaking as 'slave labour'. Taking in washing and ironing was considered more lucrative, but in an age when pleasures were home-made, quiltmaking was a popular pastime as well as a necessity. Although this section is by no means comprehensive, I hope it gives some insight into the tradition which has inspired so many to get started.

The second chapter forms the main body of the book. In selecting the contemporary artists I have aimed to show a wide variety in terms of technique, type and scale of work, and personal ability. Not all have been to art school or earn a living by their work; many have to juggle quiltmaking with family commitments. My interest in quiltmaking is almost entirely that of design. Perfect technique, although considered an important measure for judging a quilt, does not compensate for lack of originality although it is important to be able to convey your ideas in fabric. By showing that interesting quilts can be created regardless of training or status, I hope to encourage the beginner and provide interest for the more experienced.

Since I wrote *The Complete Book of Quiltmaking*, there has been a discernible change in attitude towards quilt design, with more emphasis on a freer approach and the use of a wider range of materials hitherto considered unsuitable. The importance of personal observation based on drawing is repeatedly expressed, together with the value of photographically recording reference material. Although this section concentrates on the creative aspect – the development of ideas and the process of transforming them into fabric – where an artist uses a technique specific to them, as for example Liz Bruce does with stencilled images, this is also described.

Generally, the basic techniques are discussed in the last chapter. This section is primarily aimed for the beginner who, having read the book, would like some idea of how to start; it is also intended to clarify many of the techniques mentioned previously. The methods illustrated are intended to provide a framework in which you will be able to explore your own ideas.

Sandra Lousada, her assistant Clare Paxton and myself have travelled many miles to visit quiltmakers at work, from Devon to Northumberland, Wales to Suffolk – and sometimes back again to capture a finished quilt. We have spent several days with each artist, but the lengthy nature of making a quilt means that we are only able to offer a tantalizing glimpse into their world.

I would like to take this opportunity to thank everyone whose work has appeared in this book and who has generously given their time and expertise to make this project possible. Besides illustrating the creative potential of quiltmaking, the diversity of attitudes and ideas has made it a challenging and exciting book to produce. We have been inspired, and I hope you will be too.

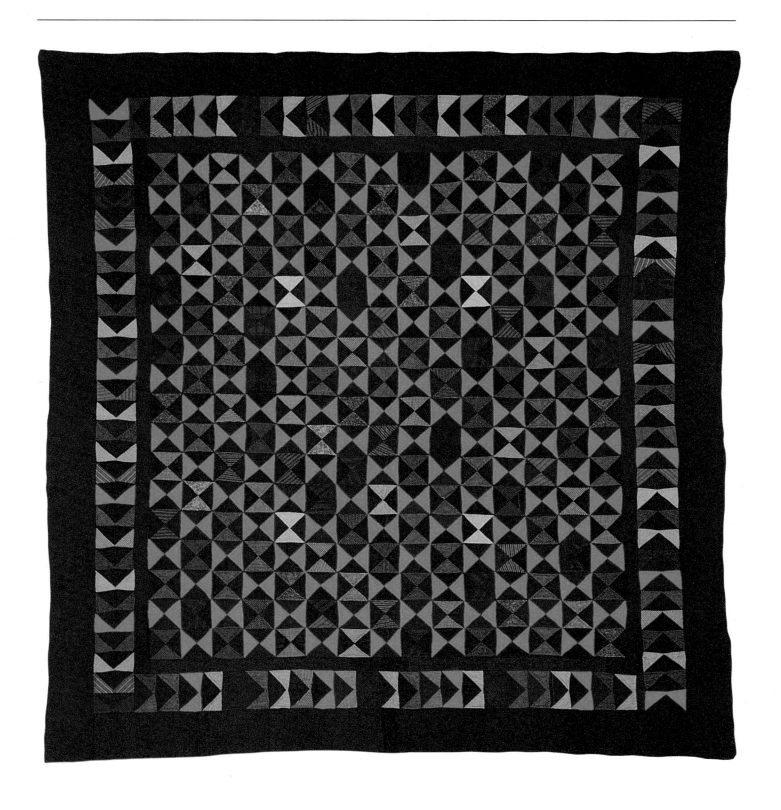

Above Bow Ties *with Goose Chase border. c.1900. 211×229 cm/83×90 in. Red flannel and woollen fabrics; quilted.*
Opposite page Framed Bow Tie. Welsh. c.1900. 183×203 cm/72×80 in. Woollen fabrics; quilted.

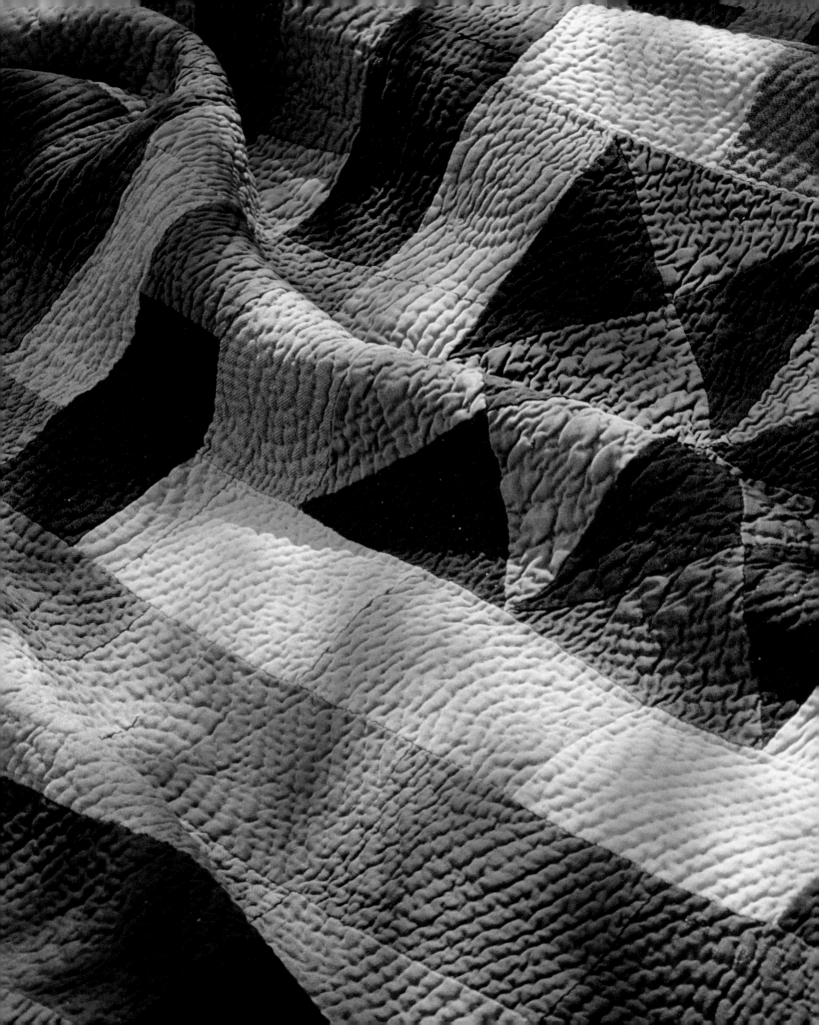

CHAPTER I

TRADITIONAL QUILTMAKING

In this chapter I have returned to the grass-roots and visited several quilters to see the part that making quilts has played in their lives. Some of these women, such as Jane Snaith, made quilts for their own use and pleasure, while others, like Katy Lewis, treated the craft as a profession. Mary Fairless, too, marked quilts for a living. They represent the end of the era when the craft was handed down from one generation to another.

Today the quiltmaking revival is widespread in all parts of Britain, but in the past there were distinct strongholds, such as in the North-east of England and in South Wales. Quiltmaking was active in both rural and industrial areas during the nineteenth century and in the early parts of the twentieth. It was a time when families were more closely knit and girls stayed at home until they were married – they often remained in the same community all their lives. There was little travel, and entertainment was home-made. For many women quiltmaking was a pleasurable pastime in contrast to the everyday drudgery of household chores. For other women, it was a vital source of income. It was often fitted in during the afternoons, between mealtimes, but put aside at night when the menfolk came in. Husbands regarded quiltmaking as women's work and complained that it isolated them from the family. Indeed, making quilts provided a basis for strong friendships and for close mother-daughter relationships. It was an opportunity to be creative in a world over which a woman had a rare degree of control. One quilter describes 'always having a needle in hand, making clothes, rag rugs or quilts'. Another

said, 'If you wanted a nice thing you had to make it.'

Many stories told about traditional quiltmakers and their working methods conjure a vivid picture of the world in which they worked. Jane Snaith described how her mother had learned that to put talcum powder on work-worn hands would keep the thread clean. And while quilting a family would sit with their feet in boxes with a hot brick inside, to keep warm from the draughts.

Patchwork quilts, like rag rugs, were a popular way of using up oddments of fabric. The simple-shaped patches, squares, triangles and rectangles were often quite crudely put together with a running stitch, but more attention was paid to the quilting. Patchwork and appliqué quilts were also made for best and for special occasions, and more care and attention to planning would be given to these. Perhaps a repeated block would be used (they were not so popular for everyday use), as on Jane Snaith's marriage quilt. Medallion patterns with a large central design surrounded by several different patchwork borders were commonplace. The Medallion Star pattern similar to the quilt Mary Fairless made for herself was also a popular design. Strip quilts were the easiest to make. Two plain fabrics of different colours were cut into strips the length of the quilt and sewn together alternating the colours. A typical full-size quilt would be made from nine strips, and gave the quilter an opportunity to demonstrate her quilting skills with perhaps a different pattern on each strip.

Patchwork frequently had a stigma of poverty attached to it, and many people did not want to be

Detail, patchwork quilt. Welsh. Late nineteenth century. 173×173 cm/68×68 in. Woollen and heavyweight cotton fabrics.

QUILT DESIGN IN THE STYLE OF GEORGE GARDINER

DURHAM QUILT DESIGN

associated with this, although of course this was not true of everyone. In contrast to the utility quilts, some were made as a labour of love, usually by women with time on their hands. These quilts are the sort always associated with British patchwork. Mosaic-type patterns were made from silks and other precious fabrics with the backing-paper method. These are really museum pieces, intended for decoration rather than for daily wear and tear.

It is certainly the plain quilts that seem to have captured the imagination of many more women today. In some ways these monochromatic quilts seem more sophisticated artefacts, with all their decorative element relying on the textural relief created by the stitched patterns. Most of the women I met considered it a greatly superior art. A plain quilt for a double bed can have an almost monumental quality because of its sheer scale. It took a full-size frame to hold the sandwiched layers of top fabric, filling and backing fabric in place while the quilting decoration was stitched, sometimes by teams of two or four quilters, in sections along the width of the quilt. The intricacy of the all-over quilted designs is all the more remarkable for the apparently casual way in which the patterns were composed. Although the quilt designs were created from traditional patterns, these were added to and interpreted in an entirely individual way by each maker. The design and stitching acted together throughout the making process. Rarely was a design worked out on paper beforehand, although the fabric was measured to make sure the main patterns would fit. The details would always be added as the work progressed.

The desire for manufactured goods led to the decline of quiltmaking, but in the latter half of this century fashion has turned full circle, and hand-made quilts are once again being appreciated for their individuality and fine workmanship. Quiltmaking is no longer an anonymous art, and the women who a few years ago considered their work very ordinary are now sought after to inspire a new generation. □

Hookey mat (no date). 99×178 cm/39×70 in. Jane Rowntree.

NORTHUMBRIAN QUILTING

'MOTHER ALWAYS STARTED QUILTING IN MARCH.
IT WAS ALWAYS A BATTLE TO GET THE SPRING CLEANING DONE
BEFORE THE QUILTING STARTED.'

Jane Snaith

Mrs Snaith is now in her early eighties and lives in Northumberland. Her father was a hill farmer and she has lived on a farm all her life. She inherited the quilt-making traditions from her mother and grandmother. Her mother, who made quilts as a hobby, was a distinguished quilter and demonstrated at local agricultural shows and Women's Institute events in the 1920s, when quiltmaking was still widely practised in the north-east. Local people always talked about 'twilting', never quilting, and Jane Snaith describes it as a country craft.

Although she helped to thread the needles and generally fetched and carried, it was not until she was in her late teens that Jane took up quilting and sat with her mother at the frame. In the beginning she was only allowed to stitch the straight lines of quilting, or to sew along the edges of the patches on a pieced quilt. Meanwhile she watched her mother laying the 'patterns' – known today as templates – on the fabric and drawing around them with a darning needle. At all the local shows, great emphasis was put on 'hand-laid' quilts, which meant that they had been designed by the maker rather than by one of the professional markers such as Mary Fairless (see page 16).

Besides acquiring the sewing skills, Jane learned the importance of balan-

Mrs Jane Snaith.

cing shapes and creating contrast with the filler patterns to give an interesting design. Her mother quilted at a specific time of the year. She began in March when the spring cleaning was complete and worked through to June or July. The light at that time was good and a frame was kept set up in a room upstairs; she rarely quilted in the winter because the light provided by an oil lamp was too poor. Sometimes if a friend was good enough, she might be invited to help, but 'bouncy' or fidgety quilters were unpopular. Patchwork and strip quilts were made for everyday use. The best ones were stored in a pillowcase and used only for special occasions such as a wedding, when the quilt would be put on the bed for the presents to be displayed on. It was traditional to use a white quilt if there was a death in the family. These quilts would be handed down through the families, though not everyone could afford to make them.

Jane Snaith was married in 1930 but already the tradition of having a special quilt made was considered very 'old fashioned' by many young girls. She served her 'quiltmaking apprenticeship' on her marriage quilt which was patched in the winter, quilted in the spring and finished in the summer. The design was a repeated basket block alternated with plain squares which gave the opportunity for fine quilting. Although the patchwork basket needed templates, the quilting patterns were sewn freehand and depicted ferns and foliage with hearts around the edges of the quilt. The baskets of flowers and fruit (grapes) symbolized happiness and prosperity in married life.

DESIGN

'Design is like icing a cake, it sort of happens,' says Jane Snaith. The quilts that are made in the districts of Durham and Northumberland are often described under the heading of North Country, but this is misleading as both areas have very different styles. The Durham designs tend to more geometric arrangements with larger-scale and often widely spaced patterns: the 'Feather' with all its variations, roses and the lover's knot are typical motifs. In Northumberland, however, the designs were looser and drawn more freely by hand, with the patterns being allowed to flow across the surface. Floral subjects such as clematis, wild rose, ivy and ferns were popular, as was the 'Goose-wing'. Favourite filler patterns were the 'Mother of Thousands' and the 'Wineglass' pattern. The quilting designs did tend to be more naturalistic and closely worked compared to the Durham quilts, but it was up to the individual as to how she interpreted the patterns.

Jane Snaith's mother, like many quil-

DESIGN OF ABOVE QUILT

Opposite page *Patchwork medallion quilt made c.1940 by Mrs Snaith with her mother and sister. Cotton. 213×190 cm/84×75 in.*
Above left *Basket block from Mrs Snaith's wedding quilt. 1930.*
Top *Detail of quilt made in 1933 by Jane Snaith's mother. Feather Hammock border, shells and hearts. Satin.*

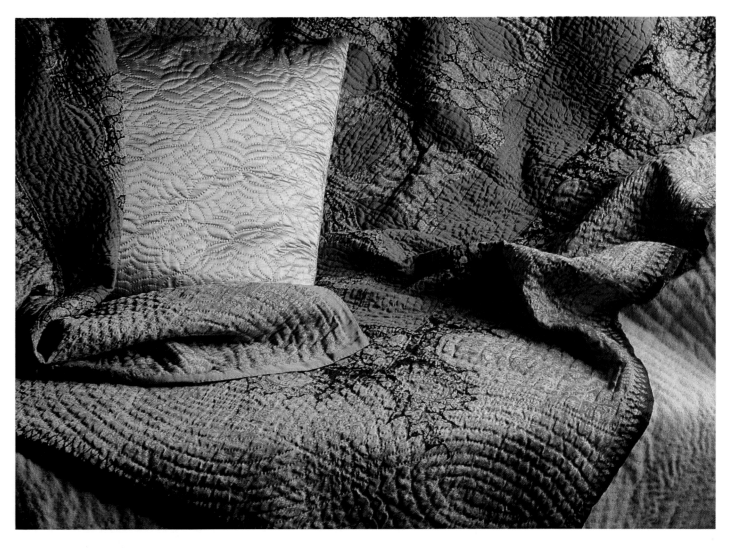

ters of her era, admired the work of quilt designer Elizabeth Sanderson (see page 16). She never copied her work but was certainly influenced by her style, as seen in the quilt shown. The centre pattern is a true lover's knot in the middle of a 'Feathered Star' with alternating heart and shell motifs between. The border shows the 'Feather Hammock' design combined with the same images as used in the centre but with additional corner designs of 'Goose-wings'.

Sometimes new inspiration would come from farther away – even from another country. Jane Snaith recalls how one new pattern was acquired:

'Mother knew a family who had lived a good number of years in Canada and they came back with a quilt they had made with a Canadian pattern they called 'Maple Leaf'. (It's one I have seen since then in books, called 'Bear's Paws'.) When they showed Mother the quilt she said she liked the pattern, and asked if they would give it to her, but they weren't forthcoming. They weren't willing to let her have it. On the way home – she had to walk a mile or so back – she discovered an envelope in her pocket, and she had a pencil, so she sat down behind a stone wall and drew the pattern while she still remembered the details and how it was constructed.'

Making a traditional plain quilt

The patterns which made up the designs were usually cut from brown paper or thin card, whatever was available. Some were made by folding the paper several times and then cutting out the shape, for example roses, stars or fan shapes. Often only the outline of a shape would be drawn and the details filled in by hand. Coins were useful for marking a scalloped edge and the top of a thimble for bunches of grapes, with the stalks drawn freehand. Some images were emphasized by a double outline to make them stand out.

A double bed quilt generally required 9–10 yards of fabric, which would be cut into three equal lengths and joined together to avoid interrupting the design with a central seam. Cotton sateen was a popular choice of fabric, though silk and satin would be used for special occasions.

The colours were generally pale to show up the contours of the quilting pattern – lilac, primrose yellow, sky blue or pink. Although the local Cheviot wool was used for blankets, cotton-wool wadding was the most widely used filling in the north-east. Bleached was preferred to unbleached, which still had the cotton seeds that showed through the fabric.

One quilter said that she always used thread a shade darker than the top fabric to stop the stitches from 'jumping out': pale thread would show up more conspicuously in the deep shadows. A tailor's needle was recommended; this was short, with a small eye and held about three stitches. A stitch out of line was likened to a 'dog's hind leg'!

Tailor's chalk was used for marking woollen quilts. Cotton or silk was marked with a darning needle (one worn smooth by a lot of sewing to avoid cutting the threads), pressed down around the edge of the pattern. The needle marking lasted as long as the quilt was in the frame.

Although there was a lot of measuring to do beforehand, an experienced quilter generally marked the pattern in the frame as the work progressed, with only a picture in her mind as to the design. After marking and before quilting, she would study the work to see the best way of stitching so that the thread was not broken unnecessarily.

Quilting hoops are a comparatively new invention and Jane Snaith feels that it was the problem of having to accommodate a large frame in a home that made the craft unpopular and contributed to its decline. Her own frame stands 90cm/3ft high and is about three times that in length. It has a trestle end and is fastened with a key to keep it rigid. The runners are octagonal-shaped lengths of wood and the webbing is attached with brass pins to avoid marking the cloth. If two quilters worked at the frame they would sit side by side, quilting from right to left and front to back. If possible the frame was positioned in front of the window to get the best light. The main shapes were quilted first, then the smaller ones, and finally the filler pattern in between. Each area was completed before beginning the next.

Quilting frames were handed down through families together with the patterns. They were basically made from two long wooden runners which had webbing attached to one side of each and two shorter pieces called the stretchers. They were commonly held together with an adjustable peg and hole device.

The quilt or three layers were put in the frame lengthways. The backing fabric was oversewn to the webbing of each runner and then wound around the top runner so that a convenient length was left to work on. The stretchers were put in place and secured. The wadding was then placed over the backing fabric and the excess allowed to hang over the top runner.

Finally the top fabric was laid over the wadding and the surplus was hung over the back and covered with a sheet to keep it clean. All three layers were tacked to the front runner and pinned together close to the top one. The sides of the work were then pinned and taped to the side stretchers so that the layers were held evenly and securely, but with enough give to allow several stitches to be taken at once.

As the quilting progressed the tapes were removed, the quilted pattern rolled up and a new area exposed and then retaped. This process would be repeated until completion. When the work was finished it was removed from the frame and the quilting pattern would rise and puff up into the top fabric, which had not been held so firmly. The edges were turned in and stitched with one or two lines of running stitches to match those of the quilting pattern.

Today Jane Snaith still sews but in recent years she has taken up needlepoint. She continues to draw her inspiration from natural subjects, mainly the flowers in her garden, and visually records events such as the summer that was famous for the plagues of ladybirds. Recently she has joined a local art society and taken up oil painting. She still demonstrates quilting occasionally, but doubts whether the tradition will last much longer. 'It's bound to die out, because patchwork and quilting, and rag mats – they came into being because of poverty. People could not afford anything better, you see they made things themselves, they used up scraps to make things. Now that people are better off, it will just go. Country people, they were artists in their own right. They could design these things themselves...' □

Above *Mrs Snaith's quilting frame, approx. 280×112 cm/110×44 in, in the Earle Hill Museum, Northumberland.*
Opposite page *Cushion by Jane Snaith, quilt by her grandmother and yellow woollen quilt hand-dyed with lichen.*

QUILT MARKING

'PEOPLE USED TO SEND ME THE MATERIAL TO MARK, BUT THEY MOSTLY LEFT THE PATTERN TO ME.'

Mary Fairless

Miss Fairless earned her living as a professional pattern-marker or 'stamper'. She is now in her early eighties and continued to mark quilts until a year ago, when she finally retired and ended a tradition that can be traced back to the mid-nineteenth century. Pattern-markers were predominantly from the areas of Weardale in County Durham and Allendale in Northumberland, a district noted for quilt designing where Miss Fairless still lives. Pattern-markers designed quilts for a living but were not necessarily quilters themselves. Elizabeth Sanderson, who lived from 1861 to 1934 and came from Fawside Green, Allendale, was the most influential pattern-marker and had a long and successful career. Her work was regularly exhibited and inspired many quilters to follow similar naturalistic styles. The designs were exuberant and flowed across the quilt's surface with great flourishes and curves. Many were drawn freehand and frequently consisted of a complex central image with a curved border and elaborate corner designs that echoed that of the centre. The filler pattern was usually one of closely worked diamonds. Elizabeth Sanderson had been influenced by and an appren-

tice to George Gardiner who was a hat trimmer but later took to designing quilt tops in the latter half of the nineteenth century. He was responsible for creating a new design style that was to give distinction to the quilts made in Weardale and Northumberland and is still appreciated today.

Miss Fairless learned to sew at school. She grew up in the country and remembers quilting at home when she was young on a frame that rested on four chairs and was set up in the spare room. She had become familiar with quiltmaking through watching her mother, who marked the quilting pattern as the work progressed. At the age

of nineteen she starting working with a Mrs Peart (who herself had been a former apprentice of Elizabeth Sanderson) and who taught her to be a pattern-marker. They worked hard together for eleven years, and then Miss Fairless continued on her own. She did her marking on the dining-room table in the cottage that she has lived in since 1933.

She designed throughout the year and describes it as 'steady work'. Usually customers sent the fabric with the order, but left the design decisions to her. The patterns were clearly marked with a blue or occasionally, a yellow crayon pencil on to the fabric which may have been silk, satin, cotton sateen or poplin. Some quilts took only two to three hours to mark, while special ones often needed one to two days: the speed depended on the closeness of the pattern, 'open' designs being quicker to mark. In 1928 a double-bed-size quilt would cost between one shilling and ninepence and two shillings and sixpence and took two and a half yards by two and three-quarter yards of fabric. The quilt design was marked in quarters and generally consisted of a border and a large centre

design, with a diamond filler pattern in between. Sometimes Miss Fairless would draw part of the design freehand or make a template specially to suit the scale of quilt. Most of the time, though, she relied on her own collection, some of them inherited from her mother and the rest accumulated over the years.

Most of Miss Fairless's pattern-marking was for plain quilts. Occasionally she was sent materials for a Medallion Star quilt with a large eight-pointed pieced star in the centre. This was a design that she had made for herself. This pattern and a basket design were made popular by Elizabeth Sanderson. Orders came not only from local people but from many parts of the country, and Miss Fairless remembers one customer arriving with her chauffeur. Often, though, they were farmers' wives who wanted a quilt for a special occasion or women who did not feel capable of designing themselves. Sometimes an order would come from a quilt club. These quilt clubs originated in mining areas (County Durham, Northumberland and South Wales) for families where the husband was unable to work due to injury, and where the wife, who was usually housebound, had to use her own quilting skills in an effort to support the family. □

Opposite page Miss Mary Fairless.
Above left Medallion Star *quilt made by Mary Fairless. 198×198 cm/78×78 in.*
Top right *The cottage where Miss Fairless has lived since 1933.*
Lower right *Selection of templates and marking equipment.*

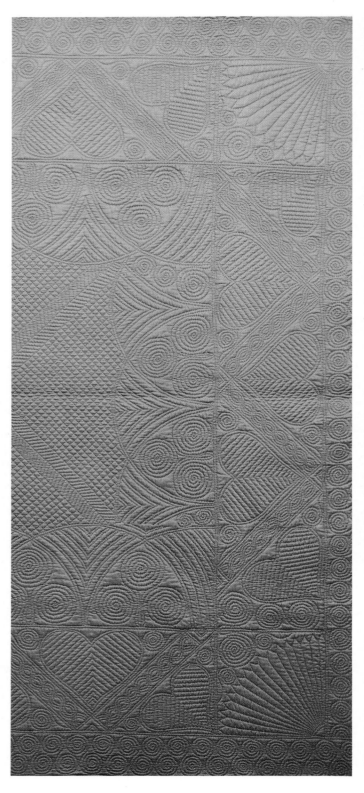

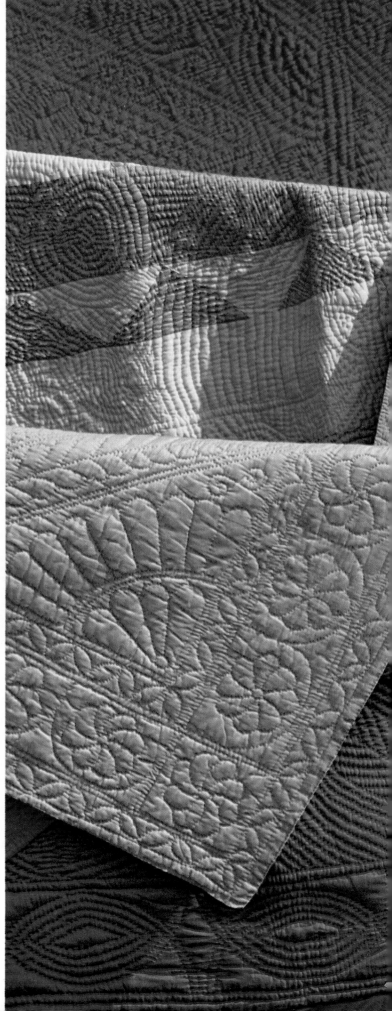

Above *Welsh marriage quilt (detail). c.1900.*
Right *Plain coloured Welsh quilts, made c.1920–1930.*
Cotton sateen.

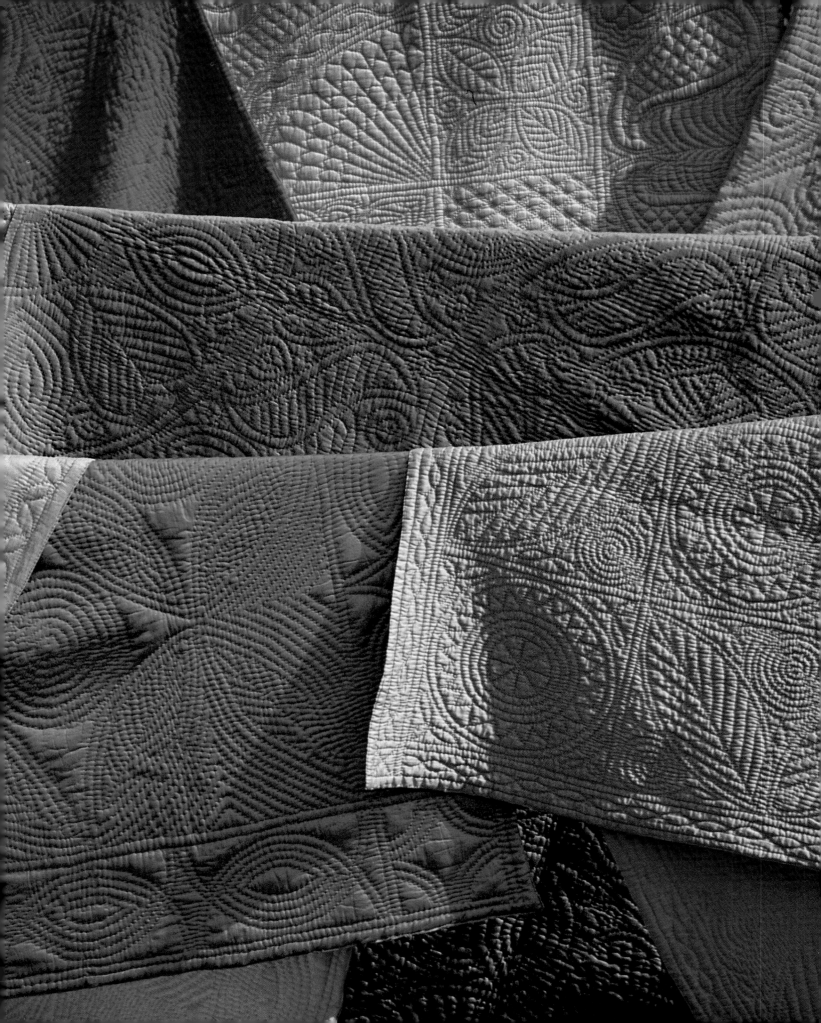

WELSH QUILTING

'WE WORKED IN ALL LIGHTS FOR A FULL QUILT.
A WEEK OR A WEEK AND A HALF,
ALL ACCORDING TO HOW CLOSE THE DESIGN WAS.'

Katy Lewis

Mrs Lewis is a Welsh quilter who practised the craft in the early 1930s, when there were attempts to revive it in the industrial areas of South Wales. Her grandmother lived on a farm and had a quilting frame, but that was for the use of the itinerant quilters peculiar to that part of the country. They travelled from farm to farm and stayed for a week or two to make quilts for the household. Usually they appeared after sheep-shearing time so that they could use the wool for the filling.

Mrs Lewis was born in Abertridwr, a few miles from Cardiff, and is now in her mid-seventies. She was taught by a Miss Owen who was also a dressmaker and had been asked to set up quilting classes by The Rural Industries Bureau in order to give employment to depressed areas. The pay was poor and many women dropped out, but Katy Lewis and three friends remained quilting together for a number of years. She cannot recall exactly when she started, but remembers quilting in the Wesleyan Chapel when Ramsay MacDonald won the election in May 1929.

The four of them worked together at a large frame, two sitting on either side and always in the same position. One pair had the better light, but the others were closer to the fire! They got on well and made design decisions as the work progressed in the frame, having done quite a lot of preplanning

and measuring beforehand. They made quilts to order, mainly for wealthy London and Cardiff clients that they never met. One commission was to make sets of quilts and matching pillows for Claridges Hotel in London. The choice of design was left to the quilter, although it was stipulated that they had to use traditional Welsh patterns. Unfortunately the majority of quiltmakers never signed their work and so it remained an anonymous art until recently. Katy Lewis and her quilting friends had little contact with other groups, although during the '30s, to-

gether with other Welsh craftspeople, they would demonstrate in a store in Cardiff to attract some local customers. In 1937 they received a diploma for their work shown at the Paris Exhibition.

The pay for quiltmakers was poor, about two-and-fourpence a square foot, but they had no idea how much the quilts were sold to the customers for. When the four were working together, a double-bed-size quilt took between a week and ten days to complete. The materials and measurements were sent with each order but the quilters provided and prepared the sheep's wool for the filling.

The method of making a plain quilt varied according to the maker. Katy Lewis marked the pattern with white tailor's chalk and always chose a thread that matched the colour of the backing fabric, as the top stitches were always neater. When the four were quilting together a long length of thread would be cut and one would stitch as far as she could reach and then hand it over for the quilter sitting opposite to continue. It was impossible to see where one finished and the other began. A 'needleful' described taking 6–8 stitches on the needle before pulling the thread through.

Similar patterns appeared in quilts regardless of regional differences, but it is fairly easy to distinguish the Welsh quilts from others. Feather patterns were not so popular and generally the work seems more vigorous and geometric in style. Many of the quilt patterns have the sculptural quality of carved stone and the designs are spontaneous and have a refreshing individuality. Large, flat and veined leaf shapes were popular, together with the 'Welsh Pear' (Paisley), hearts – not necessarily on marriage quilts – 'Church Windows' and the spiral. The Welsh quilt frequently had several border designs all held in geometric frames that enclosed the centre pattern.

The earlier Welsh quilts, both plain and patchwork, showed a preference for sombre colours – navy blue, maroon, purple and brown. These were 'lifted' with the occasional patch of red flannel or leftovers from a Paisley shawl. The materials tended to be heavyweight and with a woollen filling or an old blanket inside the quilts made warm bedcovers, although the cotton ones gave a better opportunity to show off quilting patterns and skills. Quilting seemed more popular than patchwork, but the pieced quilts show a confident and sophisticated use of colour and design comparable to the Amish quilts from America.

Katy Lewis made only plain quilts. She began teaching in 1938 and continued during the war in Abertridwr, although materials were in short supply. Today she prefers to work on smaller needlecraft projects but is still an active member in her local quilting group in Penyrheol, where she demonstrates and encourages the younger members. □

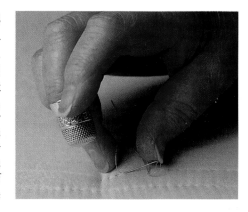

DESIGN OF KATY LEWIS'S QUILT

Right Mrs Katy Lewis. **Top** Position of quilting hand.
Opposite page Detail of quilt showing Abertridwr Star.

CHAPTER 2

CONTEMPORARY QUILTMAKING

Quiltmakers today, like those of the past, are motivated by individual concerns but all share a passion for fabrics and sewing and find that it is the medium in which their ideas are best represented and that they can best relate to. A quilt is no longer necessarily a bedcover. Techniques are 'borrowed' to make art objects, wall decorations or pictures; while those with an art-school background give new impetus to the medium, uninhibited by conventional methods.

The chapter begins with 'Folded Patterns' which is a brief account of my own work exploring different aspects of using fabric – pleating, for example. This is followed by 'Pieced Pictures' in which Jean Sheers has evolved a technique to suit her vision of patchwork studies with an architectural theme. 'Batik Texture' is next and describes the work of Eiluned Edwards, a recent art-school graduate whose work is inspired by architectural and industrial landscapes and combines batik dyeing with patchwork. In complete contrast is the work of Deirdre Amsden, entitled 'Pattern and Tone'. These quilts are quintessentially English with the use of one-patch patterns and printed dress fabrics. 'Appliqué Pictures' follows and illustrates Janet Bolton's small-scale fabric pictures, imaginatively transforming everyday scenes using hand-stitched appliqué. 'Mosaic Patchwork' describes the backing-paper technique that Lucinda Gane uses and she shares with Gillian Horn (whose work can be seen later in 'Challenging Fabrics') a passion for ethnic textiles. 'Stencilled Images' shows the pictorial quilts of Liz Bruce who, in contrast, is inspired by domestic trappings from the 1950s and the present consumer society. Pauline Burbidge follows with 'Fabric Collage', her freer and more expressive approach based on paper collage images. 'Machine Appliqué' describes Linda Straw's technique combining appliqué, quilting and embroidery and shows her making the award-winning quilt *1588 and All That*. This is followed by 'Stitched Collage', the work of Lucy Goffin, which also includes her most recent 'Fleetwood' commission. Jo Budd, like Lucy, is influenced in subject matter by her proximity to the sea and fishing ports: 'Painting with Fabric' discusses a quest for greater freedom within her work and for handling fabric in a more painterly context. 'Hand-Sewn Patchwork' describes the working method of Japanese quiltmaker Setsuko Obi, who lives in Britain. Although she works close to the patchwork tradition, her handling of colours and fabrics is exemplary of the Japanese reverence for textiles. The chapter finishes with 'Strip Piecing' and shows how Mary Fogg describes in quilt form her trip to the Red Desert in central Australia. □

Detail, Dry Dock. Jo Budd. (See page 121)

FOLDED PATTERNS

'A PERFECT COPY WILL UNFORTUNATELY NEVER CAPTURE THE SPONTANEITY OF THE ORIGINAL AND IS A POOR LEGACY FOR SUCCEEDING QUILTMAKERS.'

Michele Walker

I attended art college in the late 1960s and studied graphic design, which I have continued to practise interspersed with periods of quilt-making, lecturing and producing books on the subject. Even before making quilts I had accumulated a large collection of textiles and fabrics, left-overs from dressmaking or bought just because something had caught my eye. My first introduction to quiltmaking was encouraged by seeing the work of a friend who made appliqué quilts for her family. At that time, the mid-1970s, books on the subject were fairly scarce and were firmly and rather unimaginatively rooted in the traditional methods. I felt daunted by the backing-paper method (I still have an unfinished quilt in the drawer) and uninspired by mosaic designs, which seem to require trillions of small hexagons all sewn by hand. That outlook was soon to change.

INFLUENCES

Looking back to that period I can trace several influential factors which encouraged me to get started making quilts.

My life changed course, and in 1976 I spent six months living in Canada. During that period I saw many quilts and visited textile exhibitions showing both traditional and contemporary work. I also had enough free time to complete my first quilt, based on a repeated block. Although the design was fairly traditional the construction was somewhat unorthodox. The patches were mainly stuck together from the back with iron-on interfacing and held together on the front by cross-stitching.

The sewing technique obviously needed attention, but nothing could deter my excitement at having discovered a way of pattern-making with multiple geometric images on a large scale using fabrics. It seemed to combine everything I most enjoyed doing.

This new discovery became even more significant on my return to England, which coincided with the showing of 'American Pieced Quilts', a touring exhibition arranged by Gail van der Hoof and Jonathan Holstein of antique quilts from their collection. For me and also for several of the quiltmakers featured in the following pages, that exhibition was a major influence in arousing our visual interest in the subject. Although the quilts had the familiarity of a domestic object, each had been selected for its visual image and they hung like paintings in a gallery more noted for its Fine Art exhibitions. Stitching and craft expertise was unimportant; it was the visual impact of the exhibition that was overwhelming. What seemed extraordinary was that so many of the quilts looked contemporary in design and painterly in con-

Above *The author working in her studio on* Across the Seasons.
Opposite Across the Seasons. *1989. 92.5×98 cm/36×38 in.*

cept, although they were made from fabric and had been stitched many years, often a century, earlier.

Soon after that exhibition I met an American quilt collector and gallery owner, Joen Zinni-Lask. After seeing my first efforts at quiltmaking, she taught me the traditional sewing methods: first by hand, using the running-stitch method, then by machine, which I preferred as it enabled you to work through more ideas. The gallery specialized in American Folk Art and through the frequently held quilt exhibitions I became familiar with the wide ranges of styles and techniques. From those early years, 1977–80, I developed a preference for quilts that had a powerful visual presence comparable to that of an abstract painting. The Amish quilts were an obvious example, but so also was work where the maker had taken a

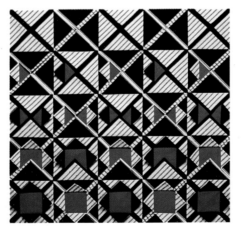

risk and, led by her own creative instinct, had overcome any problems of technique or of using difficult fabrics, which were often the only ones to hand anyway.

During this period the popularity of

quiltmaking was increasing and several American designers, notably Beth and Jeffrey Gutcheon and Michael James, visited Britain. They introduced new attitudes and ideas and thus began an important link between the two countries. This has probably not influenced my work directly, but has continued to stimulate and expand my vision of the contemporary quilt.

EARLY WORK

My work has always been based on geometric and abstract design rather than being figuratively orientated. The early quilts used simple block repeats in strong colours which were machine-sewn but hand-quilted. Although I enjoy working with fabric, the design content has always been the most important aspect and from early on I preferred to use plain colours rather

than patterns, which I feel are too suggestive and interrupt the intensity and flow of colour.

All the designs were worked out quite accurately on graph paper first using coloured pencils, or perhaps with a small-scale mock-up using scraps of the fabrics that were to appear in the finished quilt. The design was then enlarged to full size and each piece cut out to make a template. I have always enjoyed working precisely and exploring several alternatives before selecting the final design, although I realize this contradicts the spontaneous, impro-

vised qualities that makes me attracted to certain quilts which are described earlier in this book.

RECENT WORK

After a while the process of designing on graph paper became a somewhat stultifying activity and the end result became a technical rather than a creative achievement. Instead I began to explore a series of quilts originated by 'playing' with pieces of coloured paper. This presented a more fluid situation in which to design but in the resulting quilts the fabric was still pressed flat and

all the raw edges turned neatly under in the traditional manner.

Having completed four in that series I began to feel that the basic properties of fabric held a creative potential which was not being fully realized by this treatment.

The idea for my present series of work involving pleated shapes originated from seeing an exhibition of traditional Japanese art in which there were examples of pattern-making using folded paper shapes. This, combined with previous ideas of gradually revealing colours across the quilt's surface, has

Opposite top Some typical designs and working methods used by the author.
Opposite bottom Five by Five. 1986. 64×64 cm/25×25 in.
Above Aquarius 3. 1987. 79×60 cm/31×23 in.

resulted in a completely different way of working. I find that when you start a new idea it is partly based on the previous one, but by the time you have finished fresh ideas have emerged to get you started on the next. The first piece in the new series, entitled *Five by Five*, was a straightforward rendering of the basic idea. This has been further developed to create the 'Aquarius' series which I regard as explorations for future work on a larger scale.

Some quiltmakers identify strongly what they want to do before they start. I still enjoy and in fact find it necessary to work out many ideas on a smaller scale before starting a new piece. Although I may begin with the idea of using pleated shapes, it is not until I get started and begin exploring, in this case with paper mock-ups, that ideas manifest themselves, or indeed solutions occur that I had not considered. This design process can easily take several weeks and even during the time afterwards when the quilt is being made, there is still considerable interaction between the paper mock-ups, fabric samples made to size and the actual work. The colour black has been predominant in my

work for some time and is chosen not only for its own strength but for the expressive quality that other colours take on in its presence.

The pieces entitled *Aquarius 3* and *4* are concerned with pleated shapes that fold back to reveal a different layer underneath. *Aquarius 3* shows a random pattern using torn strips of fabric, while *Aquarius 4* makes reference to a repeated block pattern with machine stitching on the top pleats that reflect the colours revealed below. A more recent piece in this series, *Across the Seasons*, was an invitational quilt for the international quilt exhibition, Fabric Gardens at Expo '90, Japan.

My latest quilt titled *Jack-in-the-Box* shows a much freer approach. It is made up from nine 'fabric parcels' spilling out their contents and is perhaps some indication of how my work may look in the future! □

Opposite top Aquarius 4. *1987. 65×65 cm/25×25 in.* *Bottom* *Detail.*
Above Jack-in-the-Box. *1990. 97×84 cm/38×33 in.*

PIECED PICTURES

'LET US SALUTE THE HAPPY ACCIDENT WHEN SOMEONE MAKES A GLORIOUS HANGING, QUILT, BEDSPREAD – ONE WITH A LIFE OF ITS OWN, WHICH A PROFESSIONAL WORKER MIGHT NEVER HAVE DARED START.'

Jean Sheers

Jean Sheers lives in Modbury, a small town in Devon, and is a keen and active member of the local conservation group. The character of Modbury, with its street of Georgian and early Victorian buildings and fascinating shop fronts, is gradually being eroded by the main road running through the centre, and by alterations to many of the façades. It was her involvement with local conservation issues that prompted Jean to start making patchwork pictures with an architectural theme. At first she made architectural models to demonstrate to residents the effects of proposed alterations on the environment, finding that models were easier than drawings for people to relate to. 'My interest in using buildings as the subject for my pieced hangings stems from a hope that residents and developers will look again at their surroundings in order to extract the most suitable option for their development and decoration,' she says. Gradually she turned to making patchwork pictures for their own sake.

Combining a strong sense of pattern with an acute observation of three-dimensional forms, Jean has developed a highly individual talent for using pieced fabrics to interpret buildings and the environment. She successfully blends the representational and the abstract. In *Palm Cross Green*, for example, the architecture is realistically depicted but

MODBURY ARCHITECTURE

the surrounding trees and gardens are abstract shapes. Her style is too sophisticated to make the work sentimental — a common criticism of this type of subject, especially thatched cottages.

INFLUENCES

Jean always enjoyed making things. She recalls in her childhood making toy shops from shoe boxes with her twin sister, and in later years she entertained her own children with model buildings built to the scale of their toy railways. As a child she used to draw buildings, and had an instinctive understanding of

the basic rules of perspective.

She originally trained at the Central School of Art and Design, but her art school career was abruptly ended by the war. She remembers her college years as 'a time for playing shove-halfpenny and learning to drink beer', but she did also study painting and wood engraving. The British Museum was within easy reach, and so were 'galleries that were free and easy, and anxious to show their paintings to a young student. Post Cubist paintings by Braque, Picasso and Klee, late Cezannes and the surrealists were an education

Opposite page Palm Cross Green. 1986. 47×43 cm/18½×17 in.
Top Jean Sheers sketching in Modbury.

31

and an enjoyment. Modern architecture and Town and Country Planning, in their early optimistic days, were additional influences, particularly in respect of their social implications. After the War the work of the St Ives painters Ben Nicholson, Christopher Wood and Barnes Graham became familiar.'

It is perhaps her training in wood engraving that has contributed most to the distinctive character of her current work with fabric. Wood engraving makes it necessary to exploit tonal and textural values graphically, as she does with patterned fabrics.

DEVELOPMENT

Jean has always sewn, and in the past made costumes for the local theatre and so on, but thinks that the original idea for creating her fabric paintings occurred at a time when she found herself unable to find the right colour and texture for part of an architectural model and so substituted fabric for paint. Still making models as and when they are required, she is now committed to working in fabric. It fits into her way of life more satisfactorily than painting and sculpture, her previous pursuits; she also appreciates qualities peculiar to fabric – among them solidity of colour and texture.

Jean's first introduction to patchwork came during the bad winter of 1976. Discovering a book on American quilt patterns, she decided to make some patchwork cushions, and these were followed by an unquilted bedspread using the 'Storm at Sea' repeated block. Unaware that a renaissance in the craft of patchwork was about to occur, she went on to develop her own personal style. Jean does not consider herself part of any quiltmaking fraternity or tradition. Although she is always interested to see what others are doing, she prefers to work by herself and in her own way. She is acutely aware of the importance of individual inspiration – what she calls 'the happy accident' that

Above Cowpat Lane, Modbury. *1986. 91.5×66 cm/36×26 in.*
Opposite page The Industrial Past of South Wales. *1988. 68×81 cm/26¾×32 in.*

occurs when a quiltmaker creates a piece with a life of its own that lifts it out of the unimaginative humdrum level of the merely capable. She enjoys teaching about this subject, and is delighted that so many people of all ages and backgrounds share a common interest. Her pictures are sold widely and often made to commission.

DESIGN

Jean approaches her work understanding the 'basic rules' but giving herself the freedom to break them, preferring to interpret rather than slavishly copy. Her subjects range from the domestic cluster of cottages in Cowpat Lane, Modbury, to the stark industrial landscapes of the coalmining valleys in South Wales. Whatever the composition, each picture shows a strong sense of pattern making, and a skill for selecting and handling fabrics in a way that expresses the character of the subject.

The placing of light images against a darker background is one design feature that gives her patchwork pictures

their strength. Her main criticism of many contemporary quilts is their 'spotty' design, based on widely spaced images on lighter-coloured backgrounds. By considering the spaces between more carefully, and reversing the placement of light and dark tones, the shapes are held firmly together.

Jean starts a hanging by taking a polaroid or by making a brief reference sketch. She prefers buildings with strong graphic elements, such as those of *Palm Cross Green*, but is able to turn quite nondescript components into attractive compositions. The style of the building is obviously the most important consideration, and she notes any distinguishing features, as well as the darkest and lightest tonal areas. Familiarity with local building styles usually makes any further preliminary drawings unnecessary, and at this stage she begins sorting out the cotton fabrics. Generally, plain colours and geometric prints are used for the architecture and floral prints for more naturalistic elements. The design of borders and background is usually broached later, once the main

section has been completed. Scale is the first consideration, and when this has been decided Jean will probably make all the windows and perhaps a door, as she finds this the easiest way to plan the overall size.

The main fabrics are then selected. Using a fabric with a realistic print is not a consideration. It is the effect she is after: a wall made from a fabric design of printed bricks might well be the wrong scale, and not so much fun to make as creating the texture yourself. She often uses potato printing to give the right effect, such as that of the stone texture on *Chain House, Modbury*. She selects her fabrics with simplicity in mind and a controlled colour scheme. This makes it easier to build up the picture and avoids overcomplication.

The very strong three-dimensional character of this work is achieved in several ways, for example, by reducing the image to simple light and dark tones, and by introducing strong shadows, as seen in *Southwell*. Using a fabric with the stripes running in different directions is another possibility. Jean always finds it easier to work from black and white illustrations (and photocopies), as coloured copies are too suggestive and muddling.

She advises anyone wishing to start similar work to spend some time trying out all the styles of windows and doors they can find. They should keep everything they make and use it for future reference. One suggestion is to try making a small quilt in the 'Schoolhouse' block style, but depicting houses from different periods.

MATERIALS AND TECHNIQUE

When you first see Jean's work it is difficult to imagine how the pieces are sewn together. She has evolved a particular style that she finds best suits her designs, and considers that quiltmakers use fabric as a medium in much the same way as a painter uses paint. All her work is machine-stitched. She aims for a crisp result and to sew only in straight lines. Her basic equipment consists of a set square, fabric marking pencil, grey

thread, scissors, iron and damp cloth (a steam iron is too heavy) and a seam ripper. She admits that some unpicking is essential: 'Things do not come ready made; we have to work at them.'

Her sewing technique is best described as a combination of Log Cabin, where you sew and cut as the work progresses, and Seminole patchwork, where strips are sewn together in a continuous piece and then cut up and rearranged to make new patterns. The Seminole technique is useful for making multiple images such as windows, pro-

vided seam allowances are planned.

Jean sits at the sewing machine with an iron on one side and a board for laying out the shapes on the other. Two traps she tries to avoid are cutting out too many pieces at once, as they always seem to get lost, and underestimating the seam allowance, which then makes the strips too narrow. The patches are not sewn to a base fabric but pieced bit by bit in a way similar to completing a jigsaw puzzle. The design is built up gradually, keeping the main image and tones in mind, and selecting the fabrics

as she goes along. Each patch is roughly cut out and 'played with' until the position feels right. It is then placed right sides together with its neighbour, stitched along one edge then folded back (to the right side) and pressed. Occasionally she has to sew in and out of corners to fit in the right patch, and considers this to be the most difficult part. Jean usually begins with a window or door and uses this as the main image around which all the other shapes are attached. Generally, she finds it better to sew a building in sections.

Above Southwell *(detail). 1987. 47×88.5 cm/18½×35 in.*
Opposite page Chain House, Modbury. *1984. 49.5×35 cm/19½×13¾ in.*

Building *The Grey House*

The house that inspired this picture is typically Victorian, simple but with strong characteristic details that can readily be translated into fabric. The bay windows, cornices, porch, decorative ridge tiles, and the railings and pillars surrounding the front garden are all the sort of details Jean enjoys interpreting. Her palette was confined to black, greys and white, the actual colours of this building. Plain colours and small-scale geometric prints were mainly selected for the architecture, floral prints for the garden, window glass and ridge tiles along the top of the roof.

Using the Seminole technique, Jean first tackled the pillars on either side of the window in the front bay. A small

piece of striped fabric inserted near the top indicated the mouldings and each pillar was given a light and dark side for a three-dimensional effect. The glass in the windows was next: the fabric's wrong side was used for the lighter top panes and the right side for the darker ones on the ground floor. White zigzag machine stitching indicated the horizontal and vertical glazing bars. Strips making a top frame and bottom sill were added to the window and a pieced pillar sewn to each side. A black strip for the projecting moulding below completed one area.

Above the upper bay window, the cornice black brackets between the roof and bay were simplified and suggested by a strip of vertically striped

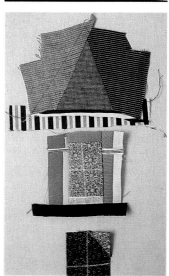

CONSTRUCTION SECTIONS OF *THE GREY HOUSE.*

Top *Jean sketching for The Grey House.*
Left (top and bottom) *Two early stages in building* **The Grey House.**
Centre *A later stage showing the corrected pillars.*
Opposite page The Grey House. *1988. 15×38 cm/6×15 in excluding borders.*

fabric. A piece of mid-tone fabric folded into a triangle was then positioned to indicate the centre portion of the roof. A darker shape appeared to represent the ground-floor window. The bay roof was then completed by adding a lighter left side and dark right side. A black band indicating the gutter was sewn underneath.

Working downwards, the ground floor window was the next shape to be completed and the two bays were then sewn together. At this point a basic mistake occurred which went unnoticed until next day. The light and dark sides of the pillars next to the top bay window did not match either the corresponding light and dark sides of the roof above or the pillars of the window below. Unaware of her mistake, Jean continued with the work and began considering each side of the bays but — unable to come to any firm conclusions — abandoned the work until the following day.

The next morning she immediately noticed the mistake on the top bay and quickly unpicked and then corrected the patches. Decisions were then made regarding the left and right sides, and the roof was sewn together to complete a major portion.

Jean's attention then focused on the right side of the house. A small window was quickly made up and a darker fabric was chosen for the porch below. The main roof was extended to the left and right and completed with a patterned fabric to represent the ridge tiles running along the top. The main sections and the sky were then joined into one piece.

Once the railings and entrance pillars were pieced, the whole thing was pressed and squared up. Jean turned the edges over on to 'sew-in' interfacing with a herringbone stitch, added lining, and decided on a method of hanging. ☐

BATIK TEXTURE

'I TRY TO CONVEY SOME OF THE GAUNT BEAUTY, TO SUGGEST THE RAWNESS OF THE ENVIRONMENTS I HAVE STUDIED.'

Eiluned Edwards

Eiluned Edwards is a graduate in textile design. During her years at Trent Polytechnic, Nottingham, she made regular visits to Liverpool and would spend a good deal of time wandering around the docks, an area to which she has always been attracted. She loves the harsh geometry of the skeletal cranes and girders endowed with spectacular traceries of rust. On one visit a redundant docker drove her round the yards, vividly recalling life 'before the heart was ripped from the docklands' and describing the effects that this recession had on the city. Much of Eiluned's work has been inspired by these visits and combines allusions to the industrial environment with an interest in traditional American quilts. In quilts such as *Liverpool 1* she tries to convey the 'gaunt beauty' she sees in the architecture of Liverpool Docks, and in her attempt to communicate her ideas she has developed an amalgam of techniques — patchwork, batik dyeing, mola embroidery and paper-making — whose torn edges and distressed finish echo the 'rawness' and character of the industrial decay.

Although she works from her own drawings and photographic reference, her concern is with abstraction and pattern-making rather than with depicting scenes and situations as such. With this interest and her industrially biased textile training, patchwork offers her a refreshingly wide-ranging means of exploring pattern-making using fabric and paper — and her techniques include layering, piecing, building up block-type patterns and composing tiny irregular and 'crazy' shapes. She enjoys the challenge of exploring the design potential within a traditional technique.

THE INFLUENCE OF TRADITIONAL QUILTS

Although Eiluned has never felt compelled to copy a traditional quilt pattern, a visit to America in 1986 first made her aware of the quiltmaking traditions of the Amish and Mennonite communities. She also recalls an exhibition of Shaker work. She says, 'I was impressed by the visual impact of the repeating patterns and the scale upon which they were tackled; the largest must have involved months of painstaking craftsmanship to assemble. I also like the accessibility of quiltmaking as an art form. There's a familiarity about it, perhaps due to its domestic roots, that makes it something to get involved in rather than to revere, as is the case with the fine arts much of the time. I enjoy the tactile qualities afforded by quiltmaking; it allows for design on several levels — colour, flat pattern (which I think of as designing in a graphic sense), and also the possibility of "sculpting" the cloth by layering, which can be used to create pattern in a more three-dimensional way. Again, I think that the "handleability" of quilting

Above A typical source of inspiration for Eiluned.
Opposite page A stage in the batik process: Eiluned Edwards painting wax on to fabric.

appeals to me. It draws people to the work, and involves them, rather than making them stand back and view, as with a painting for example. They want to touch the fabric and feel the weight, which seems appropriate. After all, whatever the applications of quilting now, it was originally for bedspreads and clothing.' Looking at the almost brutal rawness of Eiluned's quilts, it seems that nothing could be further from the tradition that originally in-spired her, but in other ways there are similarities. She is interested in the attention given to the pattern created by stitched lines, as much as in pattern created by use of colour contrast.

INSPIRATION AND DESIGN

The security of being at college gave Eiluned the freedom to experiment with a wide range of ideas, materials and techniques. Her sketchbooks are filled with drawings of station architec-ture, iron bridges and so on. She makes notes of structural features, and the patterns made by the criss-crossing of girders. The colours of industrial rust and decay have a special appeal. She is in-trigued by the building up of layers – the effects of space and form receding into the distance, and sunlight filtering through successive grid-like structures. Like Jean Sheers, Eiluned is acutely aware that gaps and spaces are as important in pattern-making as the shapes they separate.

Painting is an important part of her observation process: it requires 'ongoing critical assessment of what you're looking at. You notice more by painting because you're scrutinizing an area or an object.' She finds photography convenient as 'an invaluable *aide-mémoire* once you are removed from a particular environment.' She uses a series of shots, finding it impossible to capture the ambience in a single photograph, and seeing a collage as a more satisfactory way of conveying the large scale of the things she is usually working with. 'I also like the changes that occur as I work across an area with the camera; the light changes, something moves, someone walks into shot...there's some sense of the passage of time.' She does not work directly from either photographs

or sketches: 'They serve to feed me the sort of visual information I need but the actual designing happens almost subliminally.'

Eiluned appears not to get sidetracked by technical details – she says she is only now, for example, 'filling in gaps in my education such as learning to sew'. It is the overall effect that she is after. She works with a carefully controlled palette, using texture such as that made by batik to reinforce her vision. Although her method of designing is straightforward, her sketchbooks build up a visual reference library of sketches and photographs and illustrate the considerable thought behind each piece. She does not work to highly finished design drawings, but prefers quick sketches that indicate the basics,

concentrating on the manipulation and abstraction of shapes, colours and textures from the source material in the sketchbooks. This is followed by fabric experimentation. Sometimes quite a large sample is made up before Eiluned embarks on a full-size hanging. At the beginning of each project many fabric samples are made up to explore the ideas of layering, working from a dark to a lighter ground, colour placement and the effect of different stitching techniques. Different types of fabric are explored to see how they react to handling and dyeing. A depth of pattern is achieved by combining both colour and structural elements. Attention is given to fraying and raw edges, and holes are punched through the layers. Thin shards of colour are added to

Above Sketchbook drawings of old warehouse with fabric samples.
Opposite page, far left Stitched paper study.
Opposite page, top right Crazy I. 1987. 137×137 cm/54×54 in. *Below right* Detail.

edges, and the fabric is folded and sculpted to give depth. Fragmentation is achieved through repeated chopping and reassembling strips of various widths, in Eiluned's interpretation of the Seminole technique. Large lattice and composite rhythms are built up, making criss-cross patterns like the majestic girders that inspired them.

For instance, the quilt *Liverpool I* was made from three separate layers plus a backing. All layers were made up by cutting the fabric vertically and horizontally and then repositioning the pieces, often staggering them, to break up the dyeing pattern and suggest movement. Slithers of rusty red fabric were introduced and holes were then punched out and shapes cut out to reveal glimpses of the colours and layers underneath.

Batik dyeing

Batik is often associated with brightly coloured flamboyant designs, but Eiluned deliberately achieves just the opposite effect; she chose the method because it seemed the best way to achieve the monochromatic and architecturally distressed look that was her aim. Colours are fragmented and form abstract shapes. The dappled effect with chinks or cracks of undyed fabric suggests fragmented light, and the unevenness of colour makes the fabric look weathered and suggests rust and decay. The blue-tinted charcoals, steely greys and rusty orange-reds aptly express the feeling of industrial decay.

Although Eiluned has a strong idea of the end result, she finds the random quality of batik appealing, and is sometimes herself surprised by the effects she achieves.

The basic batik technique consists of covering areas of the fabric with a wax coat and then immersing it in a dye bath so that the dye penetrates the cloth only through the uncoated areas and in places where the wax is cracked. The technique can easily be done at home in a well-organized workspace, provided safety precautions are taken while handling the procion cold-water colourfast dyes. (Manufacturers' instructions give full details and stress the need for careful handling and storage, adequate ventilation in the workspace, and protective clothing including gloves and a mask to prevent inhaling dyes in dry form.)

Eiluned works with pieces of cotton fabric measuring about a yard or metre square — pre-washed to eliminate any dressing. She considers the whiteness

of the new fabric too stark even when only a tiny area remains visible after batik dyeing, so she starts by dipping the piece in a pale coloured dye bath to tone it down. She crams the fabric into a small bowl to get an uneven, mottled effect, stirs the bath with a wooden spoon for about five minutes — just long enough to tint the fabric, which is then dried and ironed flat.

Meanwhile, the paraffin wax has been melting in a double saucepan, and by this time it is transparent and ready for use. The corners of the fabric are anchored down with tape on a table covered with newsprint. Eiluned starts to paint wax on one side of the fabric using a large brush, but some areas are left unwaxed to give patches of colour. Once the wax has stiffened and turned white as it dries, Eiluned turns the fabric over and treats the other side in the same way. As the wax hardens, she gouges fine lines to introduce another type of linear texturing to the fabric.

Before the next stage it is important to make sure that the wax is completely hardened, which can be done in the refrigerator. Eiluned then takes the waxed fabric and screws it up to crack the wax. The clean cracks will eventually give crisp lines of colour whereas places where the wax has broken and rubbed will produce a more dappled effect. The fabric is now ready for a second colour — a darker charcoal blue.

Eiluned uses a large bucket as a dye bath, as the waxed fabric is bulkier to handle and the fabric must be immersed completely in dye. She agitates the solution for five to ten minutes and then leaves the fabric to soak for at least an hour, or maybe overnight. During this time the dye permeates the cloth through the cracks and the unwaxed areas. The waxed fabric is then removed and allowed to drip dry, which may take one or two days. Heat must not be used, or the wax will melt.

The wax is then ready for removal using heat. (It quickens the process if

Above Putting the waxed fabric into the second dye bath, and removing the wax with a hot iron.
Opposite page Liverpool I. 1987. 135 × 170 cm/52½ × 66 in.

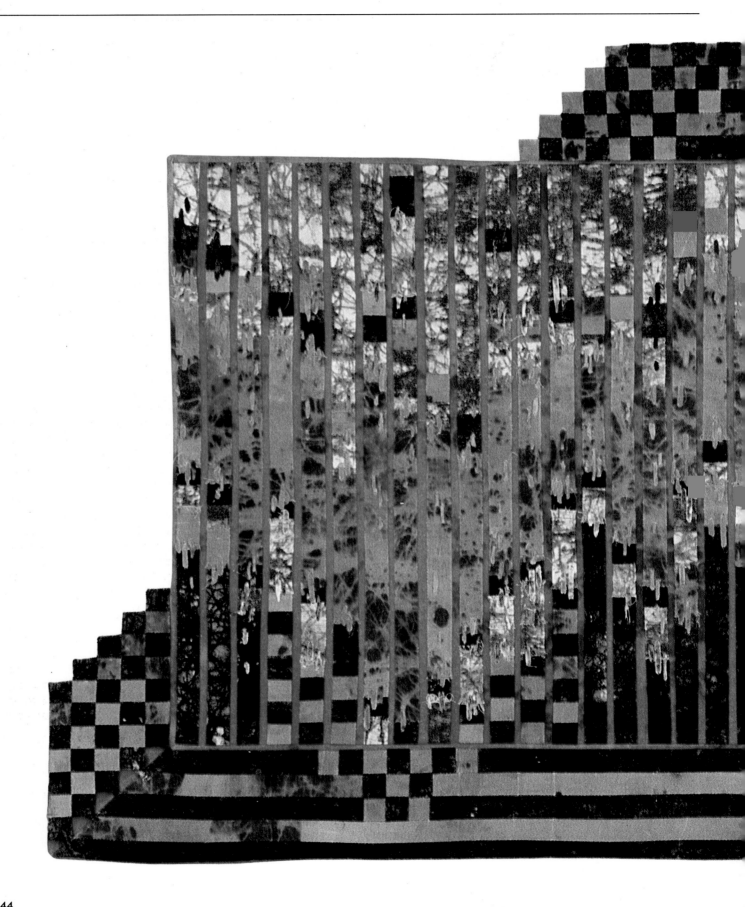

pieces of excess wax are broken off beforehand.) Eiluned melts it out with an iron rather than by boiling it out, another traditional method. 'One reason is that it leaves the fabric with a slight stiffness, a bit like paper; another is that boiling always seemed to take the edge off the colours I started out with, to make them fade somewhat.'

A bed of plain newsprint is made and the waxed fabric is laid on that with extra sheets of newsprint on top. Eiluned sets the iron – preferably an old one – to its hottest setting and begins to remove the wax by pressing down on the paper with the iron. At this stage you need plenty of paper to hand to absorb the melted wax. Eiluned finds it necessary to work only from one side of the fabric, gradually replacing the paper as it becomes saturated. When all the wax has been removed any small touches of additional colour are added by hand with a paintbrush and the fabric is then ready to use.

RECENT WORK
Eiluned has always been an avid traveller and in 1988 went to Peru, Bolivia and Ecuador. This was something she had always wanted to do, having been born in South America but knowing nothing of the area first-hand. She set out wanting to see the crafts and textiles, but did not anticipate at the beginning how much pursuing this interest would shape the trip, or the later impact it would have.

The two things that particularly interested her were the mola work and the ikat weaving from Ecuador. In fact it is ikat that has most influenced her since her return. She describes it as being crude in comparison to the silk ikats of Central Asia, and found in it the vigour and broken colours which she has always striven for in her own work but had only been able to achieve in paintings. 'I haven't ever found a fluent way of translating that effect into fabric, and I am starting to find one through stitchery.' Recently she has been exploring some

of these sewn effects, and has taken up an MA Textiles course at Manchester Polytechnic largely to gain more technical expertise – 'to learn to sew' in her own words. 'I'd liked the marks you can get from hand stitching, and had no knowledge of that; I had never really done embroidery as such, so it was partly to fill these gaps in my education and also to give me the time to develop themes that started to emerge when I was doing my BA degree, and which I felt were unresolved. They will probably remain unresolved, but I feel happier about the way I am handling them now.' Eiluned hopes her new sense of competence will protect her work from any charges of amateurishness without sacrificing its vision and enthusiasm. 'I am starting to feel much more solid in the foundations of what I am doing – I am prepared for people to challenge me.'

The piece *MRI* shows signs of Eiluned's interest in ethnic textiles with its exploration of the Seminole technique together with the blurring of colours and edges and the use of fringes and fraying. The trip has obviously influenced her work, but Eiluned still looks to her original sources of inspiration for ways to structure these new-found techniques: she feels the urban and industrial landscape she grew up in and still lives in remains the most visually stimulating – 'it is something that has always been about me.' Her work reflects the decay and renovation of many cities at the moment and could be seen as bearing a political message, but this is not Eiluned's main concern.

For the immediate future Eiluned wants to be occupied with her own work but also to continue with the involvement with Latin American crafts which resulted from her trip. □

MRI. *1989. 61×52 cm/24×20½ in.*

PATTERN AND TONE

'IF I WERE CAST AWAY ON THE BBC'S DESERT ISLAND, SWATCHES OF FABRIC WOULD BE MORE COMFORTING AND EVOCATIVE THAN EIGHT DISCS.'

Deirdre Amsden

During the early part of her quiltmaking career, Deirdre Amsden explored a wide variety of styles, but for the past few years she has chosen to concentrate on the 'Colourwash' theme. In these meticulously made patchwork quilts – usually on a small scale – she explores the concept of tone using the colouring and visual texture of printed fabrics. The quilt's surface becomes animated with flickering touches of colour which give an impression of forms that appear and dissolve. The pieces are worked painstakingly, almost tentatively, but through this lightness of touch achieve the subtlety of a water-colour painting. Each patchwork is hand-quilted in such a way as to break down the individuality of the fabrics and blend them into a unified whole.

Deirdre regards herself as based in tradition because she uses simple, one-patch designs, subtle colours and scraps – usually of dress fabrics. Her quilts may represent the quintessence of English patchwork, but in an innovative way.

INFLUENCES

As with so many quiltmakers, a deep love of fabrics and sewing drew Deirdre to patchwork. It was an embroidery course at the Victoria and Albert Museum in London in the early 1970s that awakened a keen interest in patchwork,

Right *Deirdre Amsden using a reducing glass to study* Checkerboard Squares.
Above *Typical fabrics from Deirdre's collection.*

and particularly quilting. Her mother had made patchwork quilts, mainly with hexagons, but the revelation of the appeal of quilts hanging on walls came at Jonathan Holstein's Paris exhibition in 1972. 'I saw these fantastic abstracts made out of fabric,' she says. 'I never realized that anyone could make such a powerful statement in fabric.' It had always seemed only painters were capable of creating such an impact, 'but I found there had been women doing it, all those years ago.'

When Deirdre herself attended art school – steered more perhaps by the art mistress and academic indifference than by natural inclination – textiles did not feature on the course. She specialized in illustration, but on graduating found that instead of conventionally drawing characters and situations, she preferred to make three-dimensional models which were then photographed. Although she never felt much enthusiasm for painting as such, she was fascinated by certain individual works. Deirdre speaks with some emotion about Monet's *Waterlilies* series in the Orangerie, Paris, which she regards as a major influence. She was overwhelmed by the impression they first made on her. The fact that the paintings were abstract, with no obviously definable forms, made her feel 'it was like being underwater'. When she began to express herself through her quiltmaking, she had obviously found her medium. 'I think eventually every artist finds the medium they can work in, and that's why they become painters or sculptors: it's just being happy with it. I am able to do things with fabric that I couldn't do with paint or drawing.'

DESIGN

In the 'Colourwash' series Deirdre has explored a number of ideas within a fairly controlled framework. At the time of the early works – described as 'simple little pieces with the wash of colour going from dark down to light' – it was difficult to imagine the level of sophistication they would reach, as Deirdre had previously worked in a wide variety of unrelated styles.

The series originated because Deirdre had a large collection of Liberty lawn fabrics that she wanted to use. 'The books would say you have to have contrast to make patchwork – contrast in tones, or in your block patterns – and I thought, *why* must you have these contrasts? Why can't everything blend into one another?' She found herself thinking of a water-colour exercise that was set in art school: 'We had to put down a wash of colour and grade it from dark to light, but in such a way as to leave no sharp lines or water marks; it all had to be smooth – and I could never do it!' She found, however, that she could at last achieve with fabrics the

effects that eluded her in paint.

Each quilt in the 'Colourwash' series is a self-contained exercise of painstaking detail which deploys the abstract pattern of the different fabrics to give varying concentration and dissipation of tone. Until recently all the pieces were arranged to form geometric designs, as seen, for example, in *Checkerboard Squares* or in *Colourwash Stripes*, where the patches are ordered into an overall repeat of lozenge-shaped blocks.

Deirdre's most acclaimed quilt to date is *Night-time Blues*. She has found people's response to it 'incredible'; so many of them have been able to share her memories of walking in Suffolk one cold, clear night when the sky was full of stars. She says, 'I wanted to convey the great tranquil dome of the night sky that we see from the earth, yet also hint at the fury of the universe that we see in photographs of space.'

Before *Night-time Blues*, Deirdre had always started a quilt with a clear idea of the design. This mainly took the form of

a fairly accurate pencil drawing on graph paper (one such drawing can be seen in her portrait photograph on page 47), although she did not always follow it rigidly as the work progressed and gathered its own momentum. Her ideas were always geometrically biased and often inspired by a traditional patchwork design, for example 'Tumbling Blocks' or 'Thousand Pyramids'. With *Night-time Blues* she instead aimed for atmosphere and worked from an image that has stayed with her for a long time. She describes her latest work as enjoying the new-found freedom of exploring a subject from the natural world. She now finds her work coming out more and more just from the fabrics and from working directly with them, rather than making a design and then seeking the fabrics to match.

She always aims to simplify within her work and describes *Night-time Blues* as a colourwash returning to the simplicity of the earliest pieces, but progressing further with the idea by the controlled

use of colour. She shares views held by other quiltmakers featured in this book when she explains, 'The more you explore in a concentrated way, the more you tend to find the way you want to work and what is interesting to you. The "Colourwash" theme has opened up so many possibilities that I would never have considered possible in the beginning, and has led quite naturally to my latest work.'

FABRICS

Although Deirdre may work out a basic design beforehand, it is the selection of fabrics that is the essence of her work. Her large collection is neither an extravagance or indulgence but a basic requirement. She says, 'For most quiltmakers fabrics play an integral part in the design process, especially if the quilter has chosen to work with patterned fabrics. When selecting fabrics to carry out a design there is a good deal of putting one fabric against another, adding a bit of this or that, and making piles of fabric

Opposite page Colourwash Stripes. *1987. 144×217 cm/56½×85½ in.* **Above** *Detail.*

to see how they behave together. None of this can be done in a shop or busy department store.' Deirdre is typical of many who came to make quilts through a love of fabrics. 'I collected fabrics long before I made quilts. If I were cast away on the BBC's Desert Island, swatches of fabric would be far more comforting and evocative than eight discs.' Among her collection are fabrics from Japan, France, Africa and Indonesia. Liberty prints are strong favourites, but she finds even quite ugly prints can be usefully accommodated into a design to serve a purpose.

She tries to use only one or two patches from each different fabric in a quilt since the eye tends to connect patches cut from the same material. Her advice when buying fabrics is to acquire a good range of colours and tones from the darkest to the lightest and not to restrict yourself to personal likes and dislikes. Aim for as many types of pattern as you can find – checks, paisleys, florals, spots, stripes, regular and irregular repeats, etc. Select materials with different densities of patterning and images of varying scales. Some prints are so tiny that they appear as a solid colour from a distance, while large-scale patterns can be cut in different ways to provide a variety of patches.

Deirdre always uses patterned fabrics in preference to plain colours. They give her a wider range of shading to play with and are easier to blend together, as one pattern merges in with the next. The splashes of colour are essential to the liveliness of the design and enable the seams to dissolve into the fabric without creating a hard edge. The geometric character of the patchwork is completely broken down.

Dyeing

Deirdre needs an extensive range of tones for her impressionistic type of work. She often changes the fabric colour by using one of several simple strategies. The most obvious is to use the reverse side of the fabric for a lighter tone, but she also recommends overdyeing for different effects and to tone down garish colours. Either put a variety of fabrics into a single-colour dye bath (cold-water dyes give the best results with cotton fabrics), or experiment with tea-dyeing, which is particularly good for toning down a glaring white background. Boil two or four teabags (depending on the strength of colour required) in a gallon of water for about 15 minutes. Remove the teabags, immerse the pre-washed fabrics and simmer for 10–30 minutes, gently agitating. Remove the fabrics and rinse

thoroughly, then place in a setting solution of white vinegar and water (approximately half a cup to a gallon of water). Rinse thoroughly and iron while still damp.

Putting the patches together

Deirdre's technique is traditional: she sews the patchwork by machine and quilts by hand, mainly using a hoop. When she cuts out the patches the template – although placed on the straight grain of the fabric – is deliberately set off-centre on a regular pattern so that the shapes are broken and one will merge into another when sewn.

Deirdre works at a large table with a palette of carefully graded patches (many more than she will eventually use) to one side. She pieces the design together as you would a jigsaw puzzle. The patches are patiently arranged and rearranged until their individuality is lost in the overall effect and they blend together. To check the overall impression of shading, Deirdre views the layout through a reducing glass, which makes it easier to spot 'mistakes' – abrupt transitions or fragments of pattern that stick out too conspicuously.

QUILTING

Whatever the style, quilting has always played a significant role in Deirdre's

work. The patchwork and the quilting are essential to one another and work together to complete the surface design and texture. Even at the beginning of a quilt, she will be considering the quilting pattern: 'It is important because I am trying to blend all these fabrics together, and the quilting really does help with that blending. I never quilt round the outline shape of the patch; it's always across the seams, or breaking up the patch in some way, so the seams of

Above Checkerboard Squares. 1988. 185×185 cm/73×73 in.
Far left Fabric swatches, showing overdyed effects.
Left Detail showing stipple quilting.

the patchwork disappear even more with the quilting.'

Occasionally Deirdre uses stipple quilting, which disrupts the patterned fabric even more. This is done by taking one stitch at a time, but working in different directions to stagger them; it creates a dense, irregular texture, although an overall balance is achieved.

In order to give more dominance to some of the quilting lines in *Checkerboard Squares*, Deirdre has slipped a heavier thread through each stitch.

NEW DIRECTIONS

In the directness and simplicity of *Night-time Blues* it is perhaps possible to find echoes of Monet. Another influence is in the work of Spanish architect Antonio Gaudi, who builds in an organic way but also uses small, textured fragments to create a decorative whole.

Deirdre's latest work demonstrates that she now has the confidence to abandon any preliminary drawings. Instead, she might either work directly from the image in front of her (also a recent development in Pauline Burbidge's work) or – as in *Night-time Blues* – draw on an emotional response to a situation (equally a source of inspiration for Mary Fogg's 'Red Desert' series). In this she shares other contemporary quiltmakers' new desire to break away from design-orientated work to pieces relating to the real world.

Deirdre feels, however, that although her work is showing a new awareness in the way she handles quiltmaking, it does in fact get harder to do. Like Pauline and Mary, she finds that recognition brings new challenges as you strive to keep true to yourself and to what you want to do, but also have to cope with other people's expectations of you. Because she needs the freedom to explore and express ideas, Deirdre is not at present making quilts for beds. She does not want the restriction of having to work to a particular size or shape, although she feels that quilt-making can span all sorts of end pro-

ducts, from pieces of pure art through functional quilts to political banners.

A point about which she feels particularly strongly is the need to concentrate and commit yourself to working at a piece. 'You just have to keep going at it and doing it and doing it. Even when it's not going well, you have to keep at it.' It is not necessarily that you need a very precise plan of what you are after from the outset (indeed, Deirdre's fluid approach to arranging and re-arranging fabrics shows that she keeps her options open, and works pragmatically towards an idea). 'When things aren't going well if you think, "I can't do it!" and stop, then you get stuck at that stage. If you keep working at it eventually you come through and find you have made discoveries. It is having the ability to keep working at it, I think, that is how artists actually do produce work.'

As with other quiltmakers who follow themes, Deirdre's exploration of the 'Colourwash' idea has produced some very strong pieces. It is not necessary, however, literally to work on a series in a consecutive way. 'The first "Colourwashes" I made were quite early on. You think you've exhausted an idea and go on to other things, and then maybe in a flash one day you realize you can go back to it and get something else out of it. You might come to a full stop again and take it a bit further a couple of years later. So you can work on several things at a time. I think, though, that quiltmakers who are not making quilts as a full-time commitment, or in a fairly committed way, can produce an amazing piece of work as a one-off, but the next quilt may not follow on from that.'

The integrity that has made works of art out of some of the traditional quilts was achieved by commitment of a different kind, Deirdre believes. 'Quilt-making was part of those women's lives. They didn't have all the ways we have of expressing ourselves. It was part of the domestic sphere where they could be creative. They channelled all their energy towards that one thing.' □

Night-time Blues. 1987. 215×174 cm/85×68½ in.

APPLIQUE PICTURES

'THINGS THAT HAPPEN MOST EASILY ARE OFTEN THE BEST. IT'S OFTEN THE FIRST PLACING OF A SHAPE THAT TURNS OUT THE MOST SUCCESSFUL.'

Janet Bolton

Janet Bolton is a decorative artist who creates small fabric pictures using appliqué and a variety of stitching techniques. Her inspired vision and unique approach enable her to extend the tradition of British naive folk art, and this sets her apart from other contemporary fabric artists and quiltmakers.

Her work can recall the primitive imagery of Alfred Wallis and L.S. Lowry, as well as the decoration and stylization of shapes and colours seen in Indian miniatures. The use of homespun fabrics, motifs and quilting stitches echoes that in American traditional quilts, and the application of stitchery techniques seems to derive from old embroidered samplers. All these artefacts have a special attraction for Janet. She admires the simplicity and intuitive approach to design that they display, and certainly does not consider it unflattering to have her work compared to any of them.

She is a compulsive worker and admits to being besotted with certain themes. Everyday favourites – bees, sheep, hens, cows, tabby cats, bowls of flowers, windmills and kite-flying – are subjects special to her. Although the themes change, her style does not alter dramatically. Small developments do happen – for instance, the kite shapes begin to overlap the borders – but these are more discernible to her than obvious to the casual observer. The composition is uncluttered, each shape and colour carefully positioned, each stitch considered thoughtfully.

INFLUENCES

Janet studied Fine Art at college. The course included a general training where she was first formally introduced to working with fabrics via silkscreen printing, though she had always enjoyed sewing. She found, however, that the concept of 'fine art' did not really appeal. Small handmade objects and

curios held more fascination for her, and it was juxtapositions of interesting things – especially those on a domestic scale, such as pottery, wooden toys and Indian artefacts – that tended to capture her attention. Small collections of such 'things' still decorate her house and either inspire or appear in her current work: some fish-shaped buttons, for example, recently inspired a painting. She collects the work of Elizabeth Blackadder, whose still-life paintings show a similar fascination.

At home, looking after small children, Janet found that sewing and quiltmaking could conveniently be picked up and fitted into the family routine. She drew on her sewing skills to make small bags and quilts to sell at local craft fairs. She had for some time been keen on quilts; in fact, on her marriage, she and her husband spent the money her father had given them for a refrigerator to purchase an antique quilt. It is their abstract 'painterly' quality that she says she finds so appealing about old quilts, as well as the irregularities and unexplained oddities.

However, it was seeing an exhibition of appliqué pictures that had the greatest impact on Janet's creative development. The exhibition, held at the Crane Kalman Gallery in London in 1967, showed the work of Elizabeth Allen, an elderly and reclusive lady who was discovered living in a dilapidated cottage in Kent making appliqué fabric pictures. Some were of everyday scenes; others depicted events from the Gospels and Bible and showed strange floating figures. Janet vividly recalls the strong quality of abstract flat pattern, but that at the same time the pictures were figurative. The room scenes were out of perspective but had an innate sense of balance. Although her own work did not immediately show any connection, Janet considers this exhibition – together with

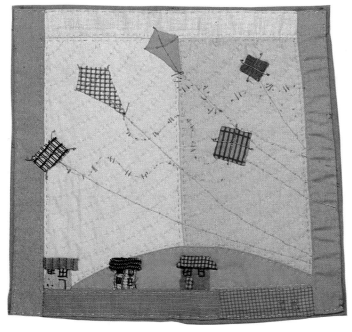

Top *Janet Bolton and her husband kite-flying on Blackheath.*
Above right Kites above the Hill. *1988. 16.5×16.5 cm/6½×6½ in.*
Above left Four Kites. *1988. 10×30.5 cm/4×12 in.*

the abstract patterning on traditional quilts – to have been the major influence on her style.

DESIGN

Janet sees her work as dividing into two broad categories. Although both use abstract shapes, one has a more sophisticated approach, with a controlled use of colour and more spacious design. The subject matter tends to be esoteric – *An Indian Garden* is a good example. Work in the second vein is more homely and relaxed, describing familiar scenes: *Cat Sitting with Flowerpots* is typical. Janet will allocate the more sophisticated ones wall-space and will stand the others on the mantelpiece among other bric-à-brac, but is equally fond of both kinds.

The essence of the work is more important to Janet than what materials or techniques are used. Composition is the key element. The basic shapes must be right for the piece to be successful; they have to balance, and yet interact to create an interesting tension. The figures and shapes Janet creates are simplified, but still retain presence and character

Above Vase of Flowers. *1984. 35.5×35.5 cm/14×14 in.*
Below *Still life of curios collected by Janet Bolton.*
Right Old America. *1984. 47×43 cm/18×17 in.*

without being either crude or seeming at all sentimental.

There is an almost indefinable line between success and failure. Janet finds that work can become heavy and over-fussy, usually when the basic composition is not right to begin with so that she overcompensates with stitching and textural embellishment in an attempt to 'pull it together'. The balance between the shapes and the amount of stitching can easily go awry. Janet admits to overworking some pieces, making mis-takes and then being ruthless in rejecting them. (This is one of the benefits of working on a small scale: many pieces measure only about 12 x 18cm/5 x 7in.) But she regards the wastage as a valuable design exercise, essential if her work is to remain fresh in approach. As well as her favourites, she keeps her unsuc-cessful attempts to help her analyse the mistakes for future reference.

She has an enviably relaxed approach to her work and considers it important not to force ideas, but to allow them to develop naturally. 'Things that happen the most easily are often the best,' is her comment; 'it's often the first placing of a shape that turns out to be the most successful.' This was particularly true of the 'Kite' series. Her practice is to work on a number of different pieces at the same time, usually exploring the same theme – hens, for example, or kite-flying. Each picture is distinct and has its own character, but working in this way enables Janet to explore different de-sign ideas more fully, and she finds that

one leads naturally on to the next. Her 'system' increases her rate of production without being detrimental to her work, and helps her to fulfil commissions. While working on several pieces she will put one away in a drawer if she gets stuck on it and cannot reach a satisfactory conclusion, only to return to it later with renewed enthusiasm.

It is the flexibility afforded by the making of fabric pictures that she particularly enjoys. The freedom to change and add colours right up to the end suits the free way she designs. In fact, the best time for her comes near the completion of a picture, when she adds her 'final touch' that lifts the whole piece of work.

Her ideas develop from everyday pursuits, perhaps walking along and catching sight of a particular view or object. She will make a quick sketch for reference, but does not work directly from it, preferring to manipulate the fabrics themselves as she composes. She is open to the unexpected: 'Sometimes doing things almost by accident will lead to new work, or people's comments will draw your attention to something you had not considered before.' Her advice is always to keep looking, and to note what you find pleasing. At first you can make a straightforward copy, but in the end you will begin to emphasize the points that interest you most. By developing these, your own personal style and language will eventually evolve.

One question she is constantly asked is how long each picture takes to make. Because she has several in hand at once, Janet finds this almost impossible to answer. On a good day she may 'lay down' two pictures. Some are completed quickly, while others take a great amount of time and attention – which she is quite prepared to give to them – before they are finished to her total satisfaction.

FABRICS AND TECHNIQUE

Janet spends a great amount of time working at the ironing board with an apparently random basket of fabric scraps to one side. She cuts directly into the fabric and 'fiddles' with the shape and position until the balance feels right. Very often she will start off a picture with the border and base fabric. Recently, as the work progresses she has

Above Cat Sitting with Flowerpots. *1987. 11.5×18 cm/4¹/₂×7 in.*
Top right *Janet working at the ironing board.*
Bottom right *A cat picture in progress.*

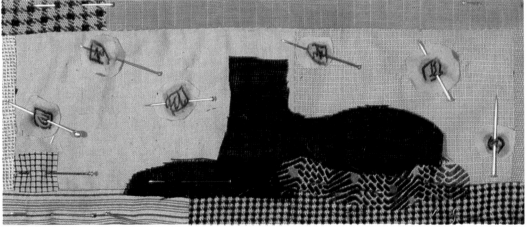

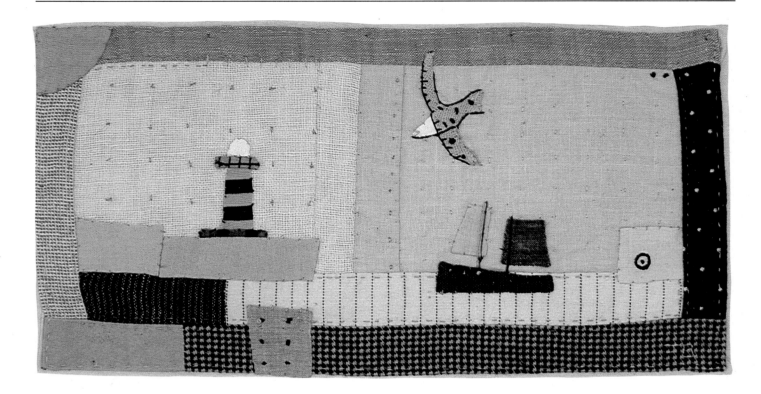

put it into a wooden frame to see how it looks, and now considers this an essential process. The frames themselves are becoming an increasingly important part of the work, and are sometimes painted and decorated to enhance the picture inside.

She uses fabrics similar to those found in a well-laundered quilt. They recall the domesticity and warmth of homespun materials and are sometimes hand-dyed or dipped in tea to give the desired effect. The colours are neither primary or harsh but a mix that favours bleached calicoes, ochre, orange/red and greys which extend to black and indigo. Vintage Liberty prints, anonymous checks, shirting stripes, spots and geometrics are all used in an inspired way. Because the pieces are so small, every spot and check becomes significant to the overall composition.

The straight lines of the borders are stitched by machine, but the rest is done by hand. Each fabric shape is pinned into position before any sewing is done. With unfamiliar shapes she first cuts out the piece to the finished size, and then cuts another with the neces-

sary seam allowances. With other, more familiar shapes, only one will be cut – always including the extra fabric needed for the turn under. When all the pieces are cut and pinned in position, Janet sits down to sew, resting the work on a piece of card to keep it flat. She uses fine Sharps needles and keeps a number to hand threaded up in different colours. The shapes are applied to the ground fabric by gradually rolling under the seam allowance and easing it around with the needle before stitching down with a small overcast stitch. This movement builds up a steady rhythm which Janet likens to drawing with a pencil.

All the stitches are a considered part of the 'show', deliberately exploited to add to the texture of the woven cloth. In fact the mechanics of the stitching is intrinsic to the making of the fabric, and certainly not regarded as a decorative afterthought or stitching for its own sake. A variety of stitches adds texture and depth, breaks up a plain ground, suggests movement and draws in details. The stitch size is crucial when working on such a small scale. Keeping it balanced with the overall design is especially

critical over larger quilted areas, for example, which could become too dominant. Janet uses and regards stitching in a similar way to handwriting and enjoys the irregularity of both styles. Sometimes she adds beads and sequins.

RECENT WORK

Janet considers that her work pattern progresses in a spiral. She always aims to achieve a balance between abstraction and the representation of the subject within her pictures. For some years she taught part-time at a junior school and always appreciated the work produced in the art classes, but recently she has decided to give this up and concentrate full-time on her own work. She points out that if you really want to do something you must at some stage take a risk and break out of your routine in order to give yourself time to achieve what you set out to do.

Although she has now been making fabric pictures seriously for about five years, she is still surprised that her work sells and is so highly regarded. Her appearance at Chelsea Craft Fair has been an important stepping stone in her

career. She enjoys meeting the public and getting feedback from them. Being seen she regards as essential. She finds it interesting that more men than women buy her work. She is now successfully selling abroad, especially to America, and is at last able to command a more realistic price for her work.

She still keeps a collection of her favourite pieces of all, and, however busy, will always find the time to develop new ideas. Recently her work has been used for greetings cards. She would like to extend this idea and perhaps in the future illustrate a book. □

Above An Indian Garden. *1988. 31×36 cm/12¼×14¼ in.*
Opposite page The Seagull. *1987. 11×21.5 cm/4¼×8½ in.*

MOSAIC PATCHWORK

*'MY ATTITUDE TO COLOUR IS PERSONAL,
AND MARKED WITH STRONG LIKES AND DISLIKES
WHICH I CAN'T EXPLAIN OR JUSTIFY.'*

Lucinda Gane

That traditional method of making patchwork quilts – hand-stitching combined with backing-paper templates – takes on a new dimension when you discover the work of Lucinda Gane, who is an actress. She appreciates not only the level of precision this technique offers (it is perfect for her inlaid mosaic-type designs), but also the fact that it enables her to combine patchwork with other activities. She does not mind that it is the most time-consuming way of stitching patches. The very nature of her work means that she has to cope with periods of unemployment, and even when she is working much time is spent hanging around during rehearsals. It is then that she is able to pick up her work. She says, 'Patchwork doesn't just fill in time, though – there is something concrete to show at the end.'

She likes to keep her hands occupied and is able to combine her love of hand-stitching with reading, memorizing lines for her next part or even learning a language. To date she has acquired Greek, Latin and Italian. She has always enjoyed fabrics and is a keen dressmaker, with secret hoards of wonderful silks and taffetas, all enthusiastically earmarked for future projects. Although her London flat is very small, she manages to fit in an amazing amount of

fabric, books on textiles and collections of antique lace and clothes. The fact that a large quilt can easily be assembled from smaller units is obviously attractive to someone like Lucinda, whose living room floor area is about the size of a double bed quilt! She also likes the idea of making something useful and aesthetically pleasing from scraps. But above all else, it is the excitement and potential of creating so many pat-

terns combining her love of textiles and colour that she finds both challenging and rewarding.

EARLY INFLUENCES AND INSPIRATION

Lucinda was brought up in South Africa, where she admits that her exposure to the visual arts was practically nil. Mention of the handwork classes at school revives memories of needle cases and egg cosies. Patchwork was taught but without inspiration. Her mother taught her the basics of sewing and introduced her to the rich patterns of Persian rugs and kelims. But it was her profession of acting that inspired and fostered her interest in textiles.

In 1970 Lucinda came to England to drama school. She began to collect lace and costumes after appearing in a Chekhov production in which she wore some original Edwardian clothes. Since that time she has become a compulsive collector of textiles and books on the subject, and takes every opportunity to visit local museums and exhibitions while touring. She has made several scrapbooks to record interesting colour combinations, patterns and fabric samples. She also includes architectural features such as the mosaic floors of St Mark's, Venice.

Opposite page *Lucinda Gane at work on* African II.
Above *Typical fabrics from Lucinda's collection.*

Lucinda was first inspired to attempt making a quilt after some friends had shown her their efforts. Previously she had tried tapestry, beadwork and even lace-making, but nothing quite captured her imagination. She had accumulated a stock of different fabrics while living in Great Titchfield Street, the heart of London's rag trade. Bags stuffed with fabrics of all sorts would be thrown out on rubbish collecting days and made rich pickings for a quiltmaker. Her first patchwork was made in the late 1970s. It took a year to make and although Lucinda regards it as an apprentice piece it is still in daily use. Her quilts now take about six months to finish.

INTERLOCK PATTERN

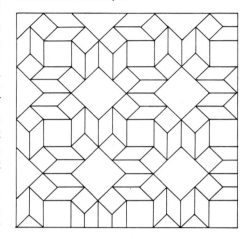

DESIGN

Lucinda considers that her quilts are of two kinds, though both are based on geometrical designs. In one type, *Giverny* for example, the colours are all prede-termined; usually plain-coloured cotton fabrics are purchased with a particular design in mind. In the other, quilts are made from scraps of luxury materials, silk ties being a strong favourite. Although in these there is a mix of rich textures – brocades, ribbed silks, satins – similar to those found in Victorian quilts, the colours and design are carefully composed, as in *Interlock* where groups of black and white blocks alternateing with coloured blocks so that the effect is not random.

Until recently the patchworks have been the result of collaboration between Lucinda and her husband Christopher. She once asked him to devise a simple repeating pattern for her first quilt and in doing so he discovered that he enjoyed working out patterns. 'Ever since then he has provided me with a stream of geometric designs like the one we call "Chinese Box" – more than I can keep up with. He provides the grid and the shapes for the templates; I choose the colours and the fabrics.'

Lucinda's response to colour is strongly subjective and emotional, marked by likes and dislikes that she cannot explain. 'Some colours I loathe, some I'm nervous of, others I love. Devising new colour combinations gives me a great deal of pleasure, as does selecting fabrics with an eye to their special characteristics. Fabric-printing techniques are so sophisticated nowadays (after all, they have even managed to simulate the appearance of patchwork itself) that there is something to be said for trying to achieve effects that the fabric-printers can't.'

Though based on personal preferences, Lucinda's colour schemes are effective in their own right. Her cotton quilts with their restricted palette of related tones have a satisfying authority. The silk ones with their lustrous texture glint and glow like stained glass, the areas of bright colour made all the more luminous by the presence of dark blues and blacks.

QUILTS FROM SCRAPS

Lucinda has made two quilts predominantly using fabrics from silk ties. One of her friends had been collecting men's silk ties with the intention of making herself a multicoloured skirt, and Lucinda began to make her own collection. It was only when she bought about a hundred silk ties in excellent condition, at 'one of those once-in-a-lifetime jumble sales', that she thought of using them in patchwork, in what seemed to be the

Right Interlock. *1988. 224×224 cm/88×88 in.*

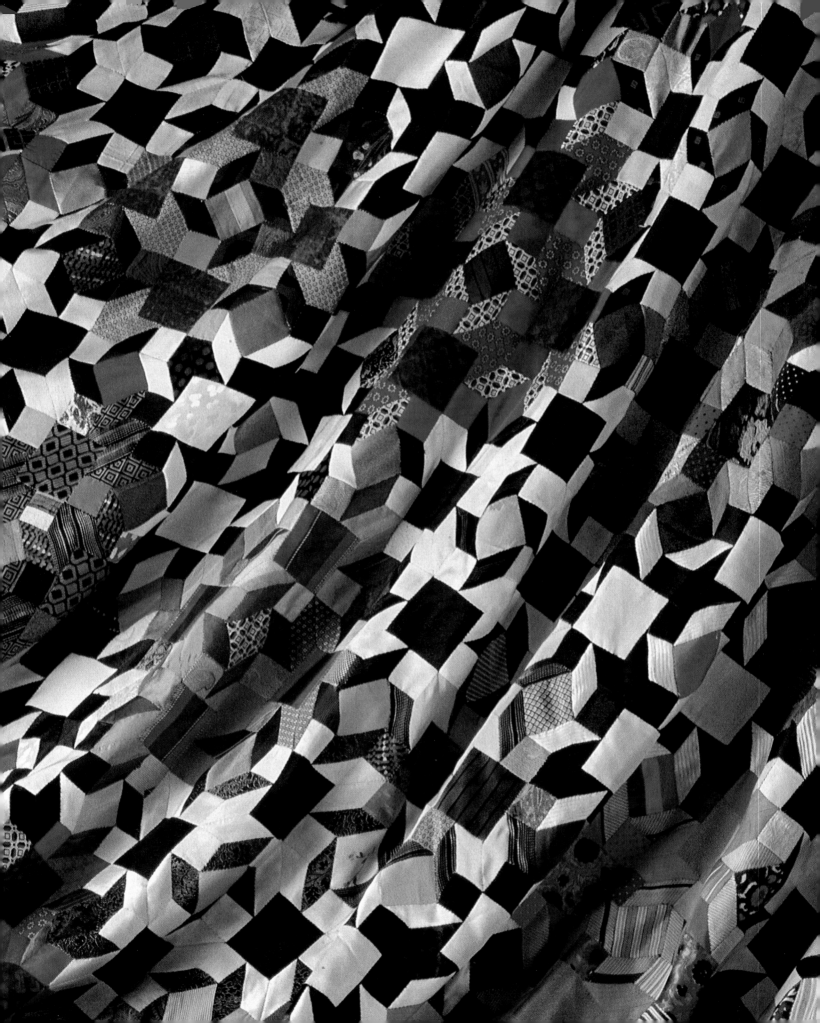

modern equivalent of the silk ribbon quilts of the last century. Her cache of ties came in a wide range of colours and textures and many had designer labels, but Lucinda bears witness to the number of difficulties attached to re-using old ties. 'They can be very dirty, permanently stained and very worn at the folds. Some come in hideous bright colours, and a great many are dark blue and black, but they are not colour-fast.' Her procedure is to take a tie apart, removing the padding and the jap-silk lining, to get an idea of its state. 'If I don't like the colour, or have too many ties in the dark range, I immerse it in a solution of Dygon and un-dye it. Some of the most subtle colours in my quilts have been achieved in precisely this way.' She also sometimes uses the reverse side, and occasionally the lining.

Lucinda used the 'Chinese Box' pattern for the second time for one of her quilts made exclusively with ties, but gave herself a stringent set of rules for arranging the colours to give a definite

grading from light to dark both within the base units and overall, from the centre to the outer edge of the made-up quilt. Lucinda found that manipulating the colours as she put it together gave her a greater degree of creative scope than completing other, more planned, quilts.

A great deal of work, too, went into the making of a more recent coloured silk quilt. Lucinda noticed that Christopher's *Interlock* design had a number of shapes in common with the 'Chinese Box' quilt. Since she had quite a few pieces left over from that quilt, she suggested that he make his new template to fit them – a suggestion she felt cause to regret during the two years the quilt took to make. 'It is my most ambitious piece of work so far, and I'm not displeased with the result.' This time the interesting textures of the ties were complemented by other silks. 'I incorporated some of the scraps of silk which I was sent as samples. I expect the suppliers thought they were too small

to be of use to anyone.'

RECENT WORK

Lucinda has the ability to create original and exciting designs from basically quite simple interlocking shapes, deploying a highly personal and somewhat off-beat range of colours. She made all the decisions for her two most recent quilts, which show strong African influence in both colour and design. The earlier one still retains a strong sense of mosaic, but there is a more adventurous combination of pattern sizes, and the use of two different borders on the outer edge indicates a freer approach. The later one breaks away completely from an all-over type design and instead uses horizontal strips of pattern in strong tribal colours with a repeated block at each end.

The fact that her work is not quilted to give any texture, and that the designs are based on fairly large-scale repeats, could make the patchworks visually boring. To avoid this happening Lucinda skilfully creates a depth to the design by marrying several strong colours with lighter tones of each, or by introducing grey as a neutral unifying colour. (This way of handling colours is also evident in *Giverny*, a quilt inspired by the colours in Monet's dining room.)

She is obviously enthusiastic about the patterns and colours used by ethnic cultures and appreciates the freedom expressed in African textiles and raffia work. She cites as examples the use of different borders within one design and the appearance of odd, unexplained patches of colour and shapes. She would like eventually to see more of this sort of spontaneity happening in her own work. In fact, the latest pieces show the beginnings of a new direction. Her choice and handling of earthy, sunbleached colours such as terracotta, orange and ochre, combined with grey blues and indigo, recall her childhood in South Africa. They are certainly not the harsh, fashion-conscious colours exemplified by the Western world.

Above Giverny. 1986. 178×225 cm/70×88½ in.
Opposite page African I. 1987. 183×234 cm/72×92 in.

Fabrics and backing-paper technique

Over the years Lucinda has perfected her handsewn technique by learning from her own mistakes. Rules which now seem obvious were less so at first, and with the voice of experience she reiterates some of the tips that beginners are often given. She advises against mixing different fabrics in one project: invariably they wash and wear at different rates, and even 'just the right colour' is no good if it is going to perish well in advance of its neighbours. The larger the patches, the more important it is to use fabrics of similar weights. Test the robustness of all old fabrics very thoroughly, pulling and stretching each piece for any sign of weakness. Pre-shrink fabrics (including the backing material) if the quilt is to be washed; dry cleaning is recommended for silk quilts. Wherever possible, aim to cut fabric on the grain. Never skimp on the seam allowances, especially if a fabric frays: 6mm/¼in is average. Finally, never use a fabric that you dislike or consider unsuitable: 'You will always feel dissatisfied, and in the end will feel compelled to unpick and replace all the offending patches!'

By using the backing-paper method, Lucinda is able to achieve a perfect fit when she sews the patches together. Each patch is tacked over a paper template and then stitched to its neighbour. It is important to cut the backing papers accurately as they form the shape of each patch. Only a few basic materials are needed other than the usual hand-sewing equipment: card to make the master templates, writing paper or similar for the backing papers, 2H lead pencil, metal ruler, cutting knife or scalpel and paper-cutting scissors.

A scaled drawing in colour made on graph paper gives accurate measurements for making the templates and shows how many patches are needed for each different shape and fabric. A master card template, cut to the finished size, is made for each different shape and from this the backing papers are marked out and cut. Lucinda recommends noting on the back of each master template the number of patches required and in which colours. She tends to use old scripts for the papers, but advises not to use the printed side of anything next to the fabric as the ink sometimes irons through to the top.

Unless they are fragile or inclined to fray, she tears all the fabrics to be used into the appropriate width strips to locate the grain. This is particularly important for larger patches as any distortion increases with size. The paper templates are then placed on the wrong side of the fabric, lining up a straight edge with the fabric grain and leaving enough space in between for the seam allowances, and then pinned in position. Each shape is then cut out with a seam allowance on all sides.

Compared with patches cut for machine stitching, these can be cut out quite crudely, since it is the backing paper that gives the shape.

Once the patches are cut out, each edge is folded carefully over the backing paper and tacked down. With squares and wide-angled shapes the corners are simply folded over, but with the more

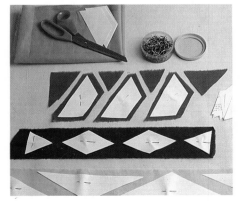 

Above *Backing papers pinned to fabric, and patches sewn to complete a strip.*
Opposite African II. *1988. 140×224 cm/55×88 in.*

acute angles of diamonds, for example, Lucinda finds it easier not to fold in the seam allowance but to allow it to lie flat to one side. The patches are sewn together with small overcast stitches: Lucinda aims for about 5 per centimetre or 12 per inch. She uses a fine needle with strong thread that matches the colour of the fabric. She finds it easiest to sew the patches into progressively larger units or blocks. She begins by placing two aligning patches together on the straight grain. She may start with a knot but as these tend to undo she begins stitching just in from the end and then works back over these to secure them. The seam is completed and finished off with several backstitches.

Each small unit is ironed before being joined to the next, but the backing papers are not removed until the work is complete – or at least until all sides of a patch have been joined to its neighbours. The borders are made using the same method, but part-shapes may be needed to fill the edges.

Lucinda favours unbleached calico, which she preshrinks, for the backing fabric for her cotton quilts. She finishes the edges by turning those of both the patchwork and the backing inwards and sewing them together with a small overcast stitch similar to that used for the patches.   □

69

STENCILLED IMAGES

'I AM NOT PARTICULARLY INTERESTED IN TECHNIQUES FOR THEIR OWN SAKE. THE VALUE OF A TECHNIQUE FOR ME IS THAT IT ACTUALLY CHANGES THE LOOK OF AN IMAGE.'

Liz Bruce

Liz Bruce is reworking the quilt making tradition of using images from domestic life to make a social comment. She says, 'I am particularly concerned with observing, recording and interpreting the ordinary, everyday aspects of life, either of this moment or through the ephemera left by previous generations, and to contain this within a decorative framework.' Her quilt *The Imaginative Cook Entertains* celebrates the exuberant dishes to be found in cookery books in the early 1950s, after the end of food rationing. A later piece, *Odyssey in the Argosy*, is a wry comment on the consumer society of the 1980s.

Her quilts have immediate visual impact with a graphic stylization of images and a strong use of colour, giving a design composed of bold, two-dimensional patterns. She combines patchwork with appliquéd hand-stencilled images. Although her visual concern is that of pattern-making and flat imagery, all the pieces are hand-quilted to give an essential richness of surface to the flatness of the printed designs. Liz studied Fine Art at Exeter College of Art, then did a textile postgraduate course at Leeds University. For many years she worked as a lecturer in Surface Design, but recently resigned from her post to spend more time on her own work,

which she considers combines aspects of both fine art and decorative design.

EARLY YEARS

Pattern-making and the use of colour were major preoccupations in her own work at college. Her introduction to patchwork occurred when she first saw some Amish quilts exhibited in London in the mid-1970s – part of the Jonathan Holstein travelling exhibition. Her initial interest was aroused by the visual power, and by the similarity that

the quilts bore to painted canvases. She felt that the statements made by the quilts were to do with the same concerns as those of fine artists, but found them altogether more enjoyable and accessible. The quilts were free from the pretension of mainstream art of that time, and Liz enjoyed the intensity of colour used on such a large scale and the textured surface of the cloth.

Her first experiments in hand-colouring fabric for use in quilts began just before her first son was born, when she and her husband made an alphabet quilt using highly stylized illustrative images. But it was after the birth that she began to do her own work more vigorously than ever before. Having a child seemed to concentrate her mind; as she explains, 'Every minute became precious, it was as if you couldn't waste it . . . I had to do my thing, as well as having a child.' Liz met several other women in a similar situation and together they began a small business making children's clothes, quilts and so on in Harpenden. Although the business itself was short-lived, she found it valuable for the experience she gained in selling and marketing her work and for the contacts she made.

From then on she concentrated on making quilts using figurative designs,

Opposite page Liz Bruce with her son and The Imaginative Cook Entertains.
Above Still life (paper collage) with cups which appear in Iced Fancies.

but stylizing in such a way that they could be stencilled on to cloth. She was able to perfect her technique through these early small pieces. She nearly always drew on images that were or had been part of her own life: seaside images were early favourites, while a brightly coloured earthenware dish inspired the *Tulip* quilt. In this piece she used two different stencilled blocks which were repeated across the surface. The tulip pattern has an appealing folk-art quality, and Liz has managed to capture the vigour of the hand decoration and the splodges of colour on the plate within the limitations set by the stencil technique. When translating a design into a stencilled image Liz emphasizes the importance of aesthetic considerations. For example, on a practical level you need bridges to hold the 'window' elements of the image together, but these also need to be considered as part of the overall design together with the way the motifs are laid out. Again looking at the *Tulip* quilt detail, the rhythm of the originally hand-painted brush-strokes is echoed in the movement of the tulip, but that block is in contrast to the simple, geometric patchwork design of the second stencilled block.

Liz has always been a collector. She has a particular fondness for '50s objects, especially china, ornaments, tins, books and magazines – 'quite ordinary objects, but with a special character that comes across.' She has memories of an idyllic early childhood living in a remote old coastguard's cottage on the cliffs in east Devon during the '50s. There were certainly no modern knick-knacks at home, but she vividly remembers the patterns and the prints of her mother's dresses from that period as well as her own, and the covers of popular women's magazines. Favourite pastimes were playing with cut-out dolls (where you cut the clothes out of paper and have many different outfits) and painting in the garden. She nostalgically recalls the festive, holiday atmosphere of a small seaside town in summer and the hypnotic quality of the light.

DESIGN METHODS

Much of Liz's imagery has evolved from her own collections, but she also looks outside the home to what is going on around her. The underlying narrative of *Odyssey in the Argosy*, with its concern with mindless consumerism and the squandering of valuable resources, is as important as the visual statement. However, Liz has a light-hearted approach to her work and looks for visual material that either delights or amuses her. She regards her work very much as an observer's response, and uses strong graphic images to express her point of view. She says, 'I have to feel what I am doing, but I am not over concerned with my emotional response.'

She generally begins a new piece of work from observations based on drawings and paintings, then refines the images through tracings so that they gradually become more stylized. 'I can work quite spontaneously with paint, but the other way I like to work is to take an idea and then refine it and refine it through tracings, leaving elements out – as a graphic designer might work. I like that, because it changes and changes it – each time you trace from it, you take it further away.' The craft aspect is of little interest to her. Her ideas come to her from her surroundings and she then works out a way of achieving them. She is, however, very interested in how the

Above Tulip *quilt (detail) with the plate that inspired the design.*
***Opposite page** Iced Fancies. 1985. 162×122 cm/64×48 in.*

technique changes the image, saying, 'I am not particularly interested in techniques for their own sake; you know, how many stitches you do to an inch and that sort of thing. The value of a technique for me is that it actually changes the look of an image. If you do a design for knitwear and knit it, then it is going to look different from if you do it as a quilt or a painting.'

The cups seen in the *Iced Fancies* quilt are typical of the way a technique can alter an image. They can be seen *in situ* on the dresser in the photograph on page 71, then in a paper collage still-life on the opposite page, and finally in the quilt. The cup shapes, which appear quite realistic in the collage, show the considerable tightening of image needed to accommodate the making of templates and repeated blocks for the final piece. (The handles are appliquéd.)

Making storyboards is another of Liz's design methods. She assembles together illustrations from magazines (often do-it-yourself ones), then makes drawings in which certain elements are taken and reorganized into her own designs. The examples shown here are

Top left *Storyboard for* Fish on a Dish.
Top right *Painting for* Fish on a Dish.
Above *Storyboard for* The Imaginative Cook Entertains.
Opposite page *Cutting a stencil, and printing the first colour.*

a storyboard and painting for the quilt *Fish on a Dish* (the quilt itself is not shown) and a storyboard for *The Imaginative Cook Entertains*. Liz's design sketch at the bottom left of the storyboard shows an arrangement of objects from which she makes a painting to refine the idea even more before embarking on the final piece. Although she has an accurate idea of how the finished quilt will look, this does not preclude changes during the making if she feels them to be necessary.

Stencilling on fabric

In her own work Liz combines stencilled images with patchwork, appliqué and quilting. The simplistic character of stencilling and its directness of approach makes it an ideal reproductive method for Liz's designs. She has adapted the technique through trial and error to suit her own needs and the fact that she works from home in a fairly small space. Her main advice is to work methodically to avoid getting into a mess!

She uses acetate for her stencils, which makes registering position much easier, and dabs colour through the cut-out window with an ordinary kitchen sponge (or a latex one, if there is a choice) and uses pigment-based dyes. These dyes are simply mixed with a binder and take only ten minutes to dry on the fabric. To fix the colour you just iron at the hottest temperature the fabric can take, so that the binder is

actually burned off. Liz uses prewashed white cotton fabric. If she wants a darker ground, she usually prints an image on white and then applies it on, as seen in *The Imaginative Cook Entertains*. The nature of stencilling makes it difficult to print a light colour over a darker one, and although opaque white is available to overcome this, it gives a pastel quality and clogs the surface, making the fabric handle less well.

She describes her technique and setting-up process. A large drawing board will do if you are working on small areas such as repeated blocks. You tack a piece of firm blanket material to the board and cover it with white cotton fabric. (Liz first covers her table with a Vinyl fabric that has a grid pattern which she finds useful for registration purposes, and easy to keep clean.) With a protective surface such as a piece of glass or hardboard beneath it, cut the stencil window for the first colour out of a sheet of acetate using a sharp craft knife. Either cut freehand, or place the acetate over a tracing of the required shape. Cut separate stencils for each different colour, marking the right side of the stencils with a piece of masking tape, and showing the direction of the image by an arrow.

Depending on your working surface, either pin or tape the fabric down. Mark any registration points on the fabric with a water-soluble pen. Put the first stencil in position and secure with

masking tape to leave both hands free. Prepare the colour, and gently dip the sponge in so that it is evenly but not thickly coated — otherwise it will bleed under the stencil. Dab the colour through the stencil with a gentle, light touch. Carefully remove the acetate and blot the image with newsprint or any soft absorbent paper (not kitchen roll, unless you want a textured image) to soak up the excess dye. Print as many images as you need in this colour, plus a few extra in case of errors later. Clean the stencil. When the printed colour is dry, register the next stencil in position and add the second colour. Continue until the design is complete. Iron both sides of the stencilled fabric to fix the colour and make it fast.

As is the rule in stencilling, some colours overprint successfully, such as black details on a light colour, but where they are not compatible, they require separate stages. In *The Imaginative Cook* quilt, the green tart fillings were printed first with the red areas blocked out, then the red fillings were printed with the green areas masked.

RECENT WORK

A collection of '50s domestic objects combined with typical cakes of that era (such as 'iced fancies' and slices of Battenberg) were obvious sources of inspiration for the quilt titled *Iced Fancies*.

Other quilts have less clear-cut origins. *The Imaginative Cook Entertains* was

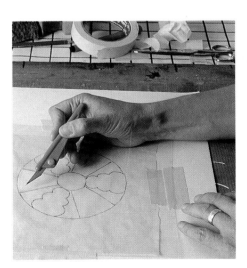

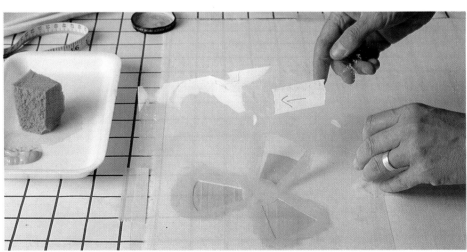

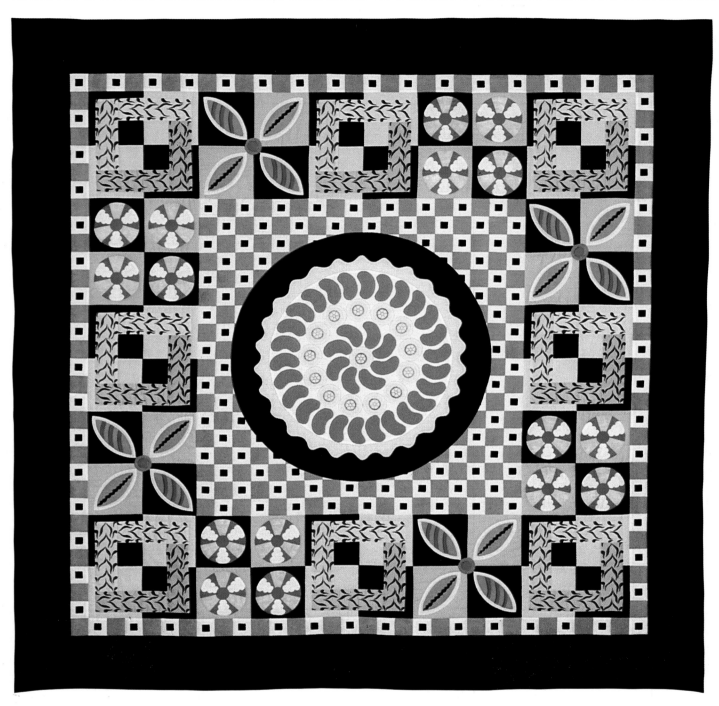

inspired by a collection of recipe pamphlets of the same period. The centrepiece represents a large flan decorated with canned orange segments and sliced bananas (these latter printed with the end of a cotton reel dipped in dye) on a black plate. Surrounding this are three different repeated block designs based on patterns of cakes or filled pastry cases. The whole design — more ordered and symmetrical than most of her later work — is set against a black, white and blue check-patterned tablecloth.

This quilt is a comment on women's work, but also expresses the cheerful and style-conscious approach to food preparation at the time. 'Awful recipes,' Liz explains, 'but there was very much

Above The Imaginative Cook Entertains. *1987. 190×190 cm/75×75 in.*
Opposite page Odyssey in the Argosy. *1987. 162×198 cm/64×84 in.*

an over-the-top feeling in those recipe books. It seems to sum up the '50s quite well. Most things had just come off rationing, and there wasn't the amount of choice we have now, but people seemed to say, "Let's make food cheerful and jolly and gay after all that dried egg and ration books and so on." We think it was all rather amusing now, but it was chic at the time – it had real style.'

The large circle for the black plate the flan was set on – an element of '50s chic that Liz now collects – necessitated borrowing a pair of blackboard compasses from her son's primary school. The cakes and 'ghastly chocolate-biscuit things' entailed detailed technical drawings to give almost literal renderings in fabric and paint of the photographic references; their decorations, like the bananas, were 'great fun to print'. Liz describes working on the master-plan for the quilt and wondering what colour grounds to use, how to compose it and so on: 'When I am working my mind often wanders off. Because it was food and a table, I wasn't sure how to structure it; I was playing around with ideas like crosses and different colours for the tablecloth. I found myself thinking of Bonnard paintings of food, with checked tablecloths and things, so I decided I would just give it a check-patterned ground.'

The quilt titled *Odyssey in the Argosy* has a stronger social statement about the sometimes absurd consumerism of the late 1980s. The idea for the work came from a catalogue which gave the most mundane items high-sounding Greek names: Apollo is reincarnated as a melamine bedside cabinet, while Triton is a shower unit. She found the concept of elevating these objects by giving them classical names and displaying them on showroom plinths amusing and slightly appalling. 'It seemed to me the height of consumerism and advertising, forcing me into wanting this or that.' The quilt design is composed of a number of illustrative appliqué motifs, some of them stencilled, all involving mythical themes and set around a central image of the sun, representing

Apollo. The group of stars depicts the constellation of Orion, while the moon at the top is the symbol of Diana or Artemis. The boldly patterned ground fabric was a '50s design that Liz adapted by repainting.

Doing her homework on the Greek myths was another part of the process Liz enjoyed in this quilt. 'I like titles. I think I am quite literary in some ways. Often I have to have a title before I can go much further with the work. Actually in the studio I currently have a list of

twelve titles – themes and titles – which are things I want to do.' Liz resembles Linda Straw in the way she enjoys researching the background to the images that fascinate her, and in the process discovers extra details that enrich the meanings of her quilts. □

FABRIC COLLAGE

'I NEED TO DIVE IN AND BE PREPARED TO MAKE MISTAKES, NOT TO BE SAFE: IT'S NOT AN EASY WAY, BUT NECESSARY TO PUSH FORWARD INTO NEW GROUND.'

Pauline Burbidge

Since the early 1970s, Pauline Burbidge has set the pace for the British contemporary quilt, and is highly regarded in both America and Europe. Her quilts, combined with her attitude of total commitment, have made her stand apart from others working in the same field. Her work has progressed through three quite distinctive styles – pictorial-illustrative, geometric-graphic and pictorial collage-painterly (her present style) – but she still makes reference to the traditional quilt by the use of the repeated block and the 'quilt sandwich' of three layers.

DESIGN APPROACH

Drawing was always Pauline's great strength and might have tempted her to do a fine art course, but her desire to work with fabric made her choose to study fashion and textiles at art school. On leaving, she soon became dissatisfied with the 'rag trade': she knew she wanted to work with fabric and colour, but in a more basic way.

Her earliest memories of patchwork quilts are of two in particular in the American Museum in Bath – The *Red Baskets* quilt, and a *Widow's* quilt with black geometric shapes representing

Above *Boat Collage. 1987. 76×61 cm/30×24 in.*
Top right *Pauline Burbidge at the Benjamin Britten High School with the quilt* Shipshape. *1989. 376×211 cm/148×83 in.*

the darts of death. Both were pieced and in a repeated block pattern. Pauline's own early quilts were traditional patterns: 'Maple Leaf' for example, was simply made in black and white. She was obviously influenced by the American tradition, but also by the everyday things in her own life. At that time she lived close to the Portobello Market in

London and saw traditional Welsh quilts and all sorts of textile bric-à-brac. She also found a second-hand copy of Ruth Findley's *Patchwork Quilts and the Women Who Made Them* and made a couple of traditional quilts from that book. The squared designs of knitting patterns, comics (including Korky the Kat) and book dust jackets all led to quilt designs: Pauline had quickly discarded the traditional image, although she stayed with the piecing technique until fairly recently, and has always enjoyed the taste of making up the work.

Basing her early work on pictorial images was unusual in a patchwork quilt, as most of these were appliquéd. In its commitment, its skilful stylization of images and bold and confident use of colours and shapes, Pauline's work was already demanding attention in a way no other British quiltmaker had previously managed to achieve.

An important early piece was *Egyptian Scarab*, a commission that considerably stretched Pauline: she spent many hours in research, drawing at the British Museum, and she had to dye fabrics in order to get the colours she planned. This was also the first piece in which the use of black had a significant impact, and this was to remain a constant feature of her quilts. The selection of colours was highly individual – terracotta, rust, ochre and slate blue, colours which Pauline still draws on today. Impressive large-scale quilts from the same period – the late 1970s and early '80s – featured butterflies, a peacock, flying ducks and an enormous fruit-basket design.

Pauline has always set herself the highest standards possible in both design and technical achievement. Until very recently, detailed drawings done in colour on graph paper were the necessary prerequisite for each new quilt, and sometimes she painstakingly made several variations before she was satisfied with the final result.

In the early 1980s Pauline's style changed dramatically, although the design method remained as exacting as before. She began to explore the illusion of three dimensions within a flat pattern. *Chequered Cube* and *Cubic Log Cabin* from this time still show a traditional link in their combination of the 'Tumbling Blocks' and 'Log Cabin' patterns. Pauline next created a series of designs based on cardboard models placed in front of mirrors to give a stepped pattern: *Finn* was one of these quilts. It was about this time that her work met considerable acclaim in America. Despite the radical change in style, Pauline remained faithful to the repeated block and to quilting the three layers together. A series of designs based on isometric graph paper followed. The illusionist three-dimensional shapes gradually underwent a metamorphosis across the surface of the quilt, an innovation that has been a recurrent theme ever since. An example was *Stripey Step* (1984), made in Hunan silk (Pauline had used cotton fabrics before this).

By 1986 Pauline was no longer finding her work a creative challenge. She felt stultified by the design process and by the precision needed in making up the quilts. It had taken her a gruelling eight

months to create just two quilts, and she felt it was time for a change. She made contact with a quilting factory and began to use one of the industrial machines. This enabled her to step up her production and it gave her work a new look. Whereas before she had done all the quilting on her domestic machine and had hidden the stitch in the seam, this new method made a very definite zigzag pattern across the surface. Together with the type of wadding used, it gave the pieces a rigidity that Pauline considered particularly suitable for wall-hangings. In addition, the process released her from a certain amount of tedium.

The second major change in Pauline's approach at this time was to begin experimenting with paper collages. These introduced new themes in her work, and enabled her to incorporate bric-à-brac and familiar objects as well as favourite pieces of fabric. They also reveal a delight in placing pattern upon pattern. Still using the repeated block, she is able to work with pattern and repeated motifs – the elements which first attracted her to quiltmaking. Working with fabrics and stitching in a more direct and emotional way allows the tactile qualities of the fabric and the texture of the stitching to come into its own, whereas in some of the geometric quilts the designs could have been painted or silkscreened: they seemed

independent of the qualities in the cloth.

Collages fulfilled Pauline's need to work in a freer and more expressive way – less precise than in earlier work, and less inhibited by the fear of making mistakes. Her experience of pattern-cutting for garments accustomed her to plotting things out methodically, and it was natural that she should approach quiltmaking in the same way; in fact, she chose patchwork because of its high level of precision. But in a way this process was at odds with the pleasure she got from drawing. In the collage technique this has come to the fore again after years of what Pauline considers to be 'technical drawing'. She attaches great importance to the knowledge gained from extensive drawing and observation in her ability to compose and handle shapes, to select and reject. These are qualities that elevate her work above that of others working in the same area. She is now combining the freedom of a painter with the eye of a designer and the skill of a master craftsperson.

Besides observational drawings, Pauline (like many other quiltmakers) relies on the camera to record images, selecting a detail that exists as a design in its own right, not as part of something else. She regards the fact that a photograph gives you an immediate flat rectangular image as useful, though it does not replace drawing completely. However, photography is quick and produces many images. It is back home in the studio, where she projects the images on the wall, that the real observation and selection begin.

Paper and fabric collage technique

For the subject matter of her paper collages, Pauline either projects a transparency on to a wall or composes a still-life in her studio. Either way, she works at an easel, re-creating the image in front of her from a selection of coloured papers used like paints.

She begins by stretching a sheet of cartridge paper about A2 size to stop it from buckling, as you do for water-

Opposite page Chequered Cube *(detail)*. 1983.
Above Finn. 1983. 236×241 cm/93×95 in.

colour painting. Pauline either cuts or tears the coloured paper – along the edge of a ruler if she wants a straight edge. The back of each paper shape is then coated with a thin layer of wallpaper paste, positioned and finally firmed down with a clean brush. The process is similar to wallpapering, and Pauline finds it best to use decorating brushes.

She first tears out and pastes down the largest areas before working towards more detail. No preliminary drawing is done, but she does find it easiest to crease the paper more or less to the shape she is after to act as a guideline for tearing.

When the collage is complete she masks it off with a window mount to decide on the best area to use. From this she traces the design. She then traces each individual shape on to graph

paper, cuts them out and then sticks each on card to make the templates. Each template and shape on the tracing paper is numbered for identification, and on each template she also writes the number of patches needed and the colour of fabric. (Seam allowances are added if necessary, for patchwork.)

The fabric, which already has fusible web on the back, is then marked and cut: this technique is described on page 148. The shapes are positioned on the backing square and ironed down. Pauline works in a methodical way, laying out each completed sequence of blocks and making the quilt section by section. Once the patches are stuck down, Pauline has the freedom to draw with the machine stitches before quilting. Some shapes butt together, while others overlap. Satin stitch is used to cover some edges, while others are intentionally left raw. Once all the blocks are completed, they are sewn together in the traditional way, and the complete piece is quilted on an industrial machine.

LOWESTOFT TEXTILES PROJECT

In 1986–7 Pauline was Artist in Residence for a total of five weeks at the Benjamin Britten High School, Lowestoft. Although not taught by Pauline, the students were encouraged to have direct contact with an artist at work, so participating in a learning process with far more impact than simply looking at a finished exhibition. It also led to textile- and design-related projects being explored by pupils.

Pauline's contact with the school broadened her vision of art education, though she found it difficult to work and create in such an environment. However, her visits to the Lowestoft docks were very important to her and produced much fresh visual source material for her design work. With *IH5*, the quilt she completed at the school, Pauline felt that she was echoing work she had done before rather than breaking new

Opposite page, top Paper collage used for Shipshape. ***Left*** *Using a window mount over the collage.*
Above *Pauline working on the quilt* Shipshape.

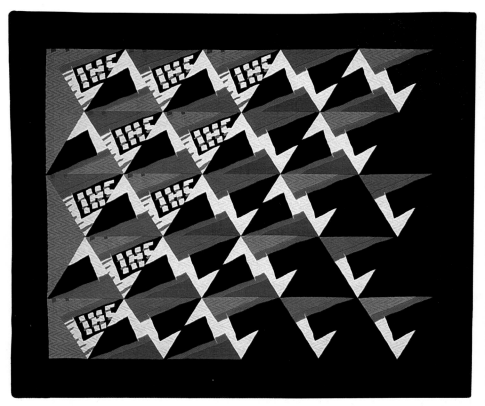

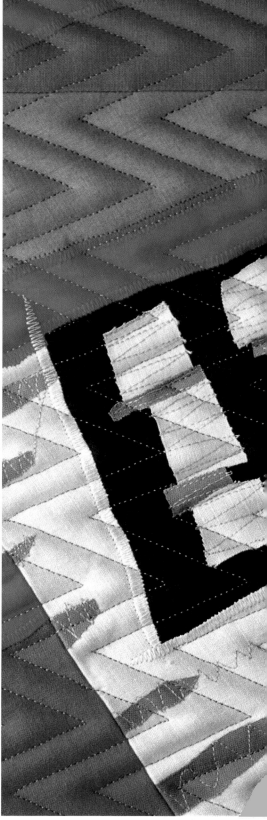

ground: 'It was very strange to have to be talking about the work as I was making it, so in some ways it is as if I stayed still at that point. I was doing things that were familiar to me because of this thing of having to talk my way through it . . . As an artist this is not totally satisfying – one always looks for a new challenge.' *IH5* displays Pauline's recurrent theme of gradually simplifying the images across the surface of the quilt – 'I wanted those blocks to change, wanted more detail in some of them, and more simplified blocks as I went along' – and in the event she is not dissatisfied with the result.

The *IH5* block also makes an appearance in *Shipshape*, the result of a subsequent commission from the school for their drama area. The *Shipshape* design, made from three different collages, shows a typical example of Pauline's work process at the time. One collage represented seaside bric-à-brac, while the other two were inspired by projected transparencies of images from the docks. Once again, in *Shipshape*,

Pauline transformed the blocks as they crossed the quilt. 'Because it was a quilt you would see from very far away and also very close up, I wanted it to have a lot of boldness to it from a distance but also a lot of detail when you got close up. So with each of the blocks I started off with a lot of detail and then gradually worked towards very open, simple blocks, in order to give space for the next detailed blocks to come in – they form diagonal stripes across the surface.' She began the design with a sketch to indicate the overall size and area that each block was to fill (the blocks, incidentally, were deliberately identical in size with those of the wall itself) then made a series of small but detailed drawings to work out the progression of each block. She made a black and white drawing of the complete design, then photocopied it several times to experiment with different colours, drawing very much on 'Lowestoft colours – the blues of the sea and the blues and reds you see painted on boats'. Periodically Pauline took samples

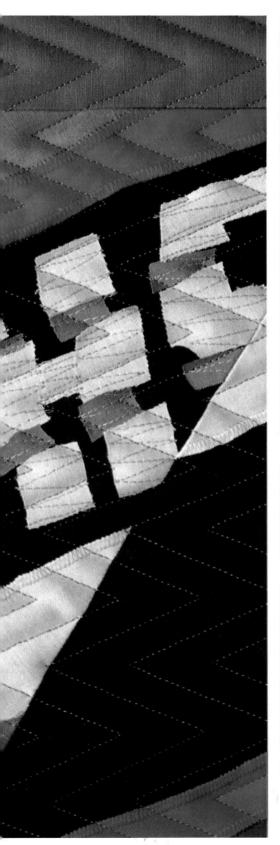

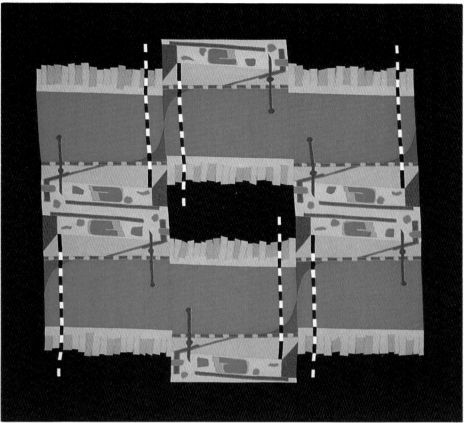

and pinned them up on the wall *in situ* to check that they looked good in the vast and unfamiliar space for which she was designing. When she was satisfied with the design, Pauline then made a complete tracing for each block, copying directly from the collage or making changes as necessary. The templates were then made, and the quilt progressed according to her usual paper and fabric collage technique.

Another quilt resulting from the residency and contact with the docks was *Lowestoft 1*. Pauline was struck by the sight of a huge boat being painted in dry dock. The paint was being applied with diminutive rollers – 'Just the small paint strokes and the enormous size of it seemed really inspirational.' Pauline took photographs both of details and of the whole boat, and from collages

Top Lowestoft I. *1987. 147×140 cm/58×55 in.*
Above *Pauline's photograph used for the design of Lowestoft I.*
Top left and centre IH5 *and detail. 1987. 178×152 cm/70×60 in.*

finally developed a repeat of six identical blocks. These alternate and dovetail together in two rows of three, creating large areas of plain fabric which disguise and camouflage the individual blocks, yet successfully convey the sense of space that was present in Pauline's inspiration.

RECENT WORK

Some of Pauline's more recent work was inspired by a book on tropical fish that she was shown during a visit to Australia. She began by working on single fish images, but went on to explore the use of a multiple image, starting off by showing the fish quite clearly and then making the patterns and images of the coral and so on take over as you look down the quilt. She worked on this idea in a quilt called *Joining Forces*. Here she was trying to reflect the characteristic movement of fish, allowing the fish image to move forward within the block and so naturally form abstract pattern.

Kate's Vase II is a quilt which grew from a paper collage study of a still-life set-up that included a borrowed vase. After creating *Kate's Vase I* Pauline felt that there was more to extract from this complicated collage. The objects chosen for the still life deliberately had pattern on them, and Pauline decided to use this pattern in a fairly realistic way in the lower side, and also used mirror images to create her pattern. On the upper diagonal half a flat pattern in two colours was used to try to give the effect of a photographic negative, almost like an after-image illusion (as when your eyes have been focusing on bright colours and see the complementary after-image on turning to a white surface).

In these pieces Pauline makes the blocks grow and change, interweaving them more than in the past so that the rigidity is broken down. 'The continuing theme of stripes is very likely to play a large part in new work, and perhaps intercutting two images together as one block may provide a further idea to break down the realistic shapes.' Pauline

also hopes to explore different ways of dyeing fabric so that the colours have an uneven quality and therefore give the illusion of greater depth in a piece of work. Her latest work is still at an early stage; she knows that there is a lot more 'pushing forward' to do, but feels happy to go along with this.

Like every artist, she describes it as being a battle to make time to work. 'There are always other things that you get sidetracked into doing. You have to consciously say that you are doing work today, and no one can interrupt you.'

EXPANDING THE BOUNDARIES OF THE TRADITION

From the very beginning of the 1970s Pauline has been a key figure in the development of the contemporary quilt, both in terms of her own output and by striving towards getting better recognition for the art quilt. She says, 'I don't want to just throw off the traditions of quiltmaking, because I am close to that tradition and love being inspired by it. I am certainly inspired by the old quilts, and I like to show that inspiration through my work.' Such a declaration cuts across those contemporary quilters who feel that the connection with a domestic craft prohibits their work being judged independently as an art form. While more and more of them are trying to avoid the word 'quilt' to describe their work, Pauline explicitly wants to continue the traditions of quiltmaking. At the same time, she has never been a great theorist, and prefers to let others do the arguing and come up with the categories. As her work becomes more sought-after and celebrated, she is acutely aware of the trap of becoming well known so that people expect work of a particular style and make it difficult for her to push forward and change direction: she needs the freedom to explore new directions and challenges, to dive in and be prepared to make mistakes. She says, 'I want to do the work that is close to my heart; that's the thing that keeps me going.'

One of the most difficult progressions

for quiltmakers is breaking from the traditional images to create individual designs. Pauline's own originality and the way she develops an idea, working on an image until it becomes a fully fledged design, is an excellent demonstration of this complex process. From her teaching experience, Pauline is able to offer beginners some advice on producing work with some individuality about it. Just as you should go beyond the traditional quilt for inspiration, it is not enough simply to look at contemporary quilts: these represent someone else's vision, which in a sense is second-hand. Imitating another quiltmaker's approach without putting into it anything of yourself results in work that is derivative and lacking in personal identity. 'It is fine to look at other people's work, but in the end you have to get back to what inspires you.'

Pauline places most emphasis on 'visual collecting' – favourite colours, fabrics, shapes, textures, anything that strikes you as interesting. 'Make up scrap books and look at them to decide if there is a common theme. Ask what it is that makes you choose certain things: colour, for example, can often point to a direction – and work on that.' She does not consider drawing essential for everyone, although it is useful for her personally, and for quiltmakers who make pictorial and representational images; you may be one of those people who prefer to work directly with the technical qualities of fabrics. It may be pattern-making, as in Lucinda Gane's work, together with a love of certain colour combinations; or a visit to a particular place, as in Mary Fogg's Australian series. 'In the end it is having the will to really want to produce something that is most important.'

Years of experience and, to a certain extent, the recognition her work receives, gave Pauline the confidence to make her great leap to fabric collage. The process of cutting directly into the fabric in response to the subject matter in front of her in itself introduces new themes into her work. In this new freedom she is creating even wider

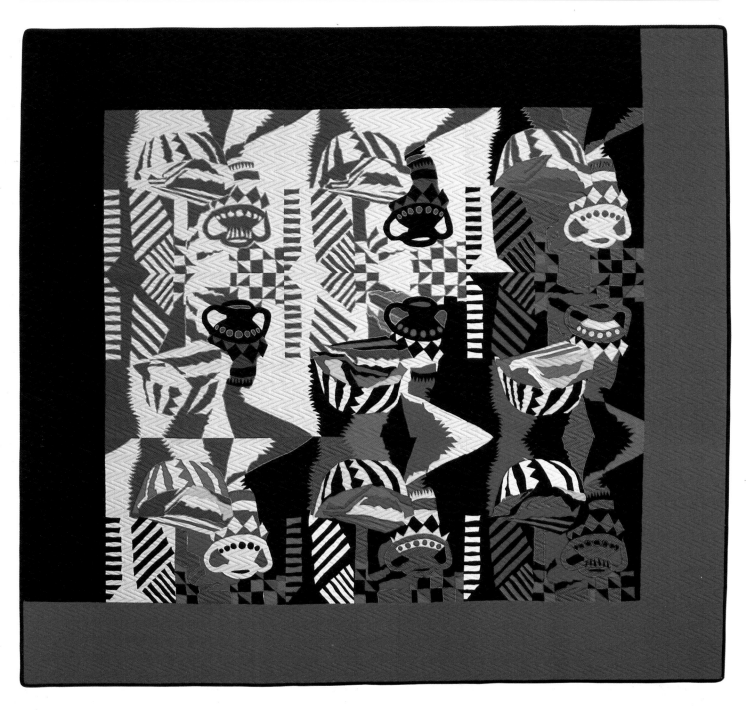

boundaries for the contemporary quilt.

Up to this point Pauline regarded herself as a 'designer craftsperson'. Her earlier work was very much that of the designer, planning a piece very exactly, an approach which was heavily influenced by the technique. Now she feels herself moving towards being an 'artist craftsperson', since she is working directly with the fabric and making decisions as the work progresses. Although the new work still shows the characteristic strength of vision and the individualistic colour combinations – together with the skill in handling form and pattern, she is now drawing with the stitches and fabric in a way not seen before, and her new work is based on emotional response. Her future quilting will be 'like scribbling with the lines of stitching, but through all three layers.' □

Kate's Vase II. 1989. 170×163 cm/67×64 in. (See page 2)

MACHINE APPLIQUE

'TECHNIQUES NEED TO BE SHARED:
THEY ENABLE YOU TO DEVELOP INDIVIDUAL IDEAS
RATHER THAN JUST PRODUCING COPIES.'

Linda Straw

Linda Straw is passionate about the embroidery that she uses in her work and combines with a long-standing love of literature, history and decorative art. She does not think of making quilts so much as of interpreting art and literature in terms of fabrics. To attempt to keep pace with her many ideas she works with a machine and over the years has developed a technique that combines embroidery, appliqué and quilting, working initially on the reverse side of the piece. She delights in creating layer upon layer of rich embroidered patterns and uses mainly velvets, satin and silks.

INFLUENCES

Linda grew up in a household where enjoyment of reading and literature was encouraged from an early age. She adored looking at and drawing historical costumes, and dressing up. She vividly recalls a toy theatre being a particular source of pleasure for her inventive imagination. Linda describes her mother, a teacher, as being 'progressive in every sense'. There were always handworked projects in various stages of completion around the house. Linda remembers a pile of hexagons tacked over backing papers, though little seemed to happen to them. Her strongest memory of the many projects that her mother always had on the go is of two skirts. One was made from parachute silk and was being embroidered with 'The Twelve Days of Christmas'. It took so long to complete that her mother wore the skirt in the meantime, and Linda, aged about six, recalls seeing 'odd legs sticking out' and that at one time 'there were only seven-and-a-half Lords a-leaping!' The second skirt had scenes from the Bayeux Tapestry embroidered round the hem, and because it was made at a summer

Above *Linda Straw delivering her quilt to the Nostell Priory Quilt Festival, 1987.*
Right *Linda working on* 1588 and All That.

school in Hastings, it had the tall drying huts depicted on the waistband.

Linda's grandmother, who lived in Durham, belonged to the generation that made quilts in preparation for marriage. Linda still has one that she made, but does not have any feeling of being influenced by this connection with tradition. She likes the old quilts – plain ones are her favourites, though she is also fond of Strippies and Welsh quilts – but prefers them well worn, showing a patina of age.

Linda has always been outspoken and frequently finds herself at odds with others over her point of view. During the late 1960s and early '70s Linda appreciated artists whose paintings were figurative at a time when most work was abstract. Her drawings were always full of people and narrative in content (as her quilts are today) – definitely not part of the mainstream thinking. Since she has been politically active throughout her life, she might be expected to be making political banners. In practice, she says, these are run up a few minutes before a march begins; she has made many herself over the years in support of causes such as the anti-apartheid movement.

STYLE AND SUBJECT MATTER

Linda has always sewn, but first started developing the work for which she is noted in about 1979. Having enjoyed making dolls, she began to make them flat and to appliqué each one on to a square of fabric. She then joined the squares into a quilt. About this time she began experimental 'drawing' with sewing machine stitches.

From that moment on, the idea of what she wanted to achieve became more definite and she embarked on a long and often frustrating journey towards her technical goal. Never one to follow the rules, Linda derived her technique from trial and error, but her progress was always fuelled by the enthusiasm she has for storytelling in her work and by the pleasure she finds in researching each piece.

A list of the titles of Linda's major

works conveys a clear picture of the periods and subject matter she finds sympathetic: *A Midsummer Night's Dream, King Lear, 'O sweet and lovely wall, Show me thy chink'*; *Folk Tales, Canterbury Tales*; *Under Milk Wood*; *1588 and All That*. Art Nouveau and the Victorian age featured in her early work, but then she turned to the Middle Ages – an era she regards as more enjoyable. Motifs from the *Book of Kells* and hunting scenes are recurrent themes, and she likes to include jokes when the opportunity arises. The figures have a strong, colourful character, often Brueghel-like, with a ribald Chaucerian sense of humour. The Elizabethan age provided rich inspiration for *1588 and All That* and illustrates Linda's capacity to mix a wide variety of

different elements within a piece.

Apart from references to literature, art and history, Linda is influenced by the styles of illustrators such as Arthur Rackham, Edmund Dulac and Walter Crane. She relishes the embellishment and pure decoration of their work. William Morris and the Arts and Crafts movement have also had a major effect on her work. A more contemporary influence has been the painter Stanley Spencer, and his use of decoration in his pictures: this is particularly felt in some of the characterization of scenes in Linda's *Under Milk Wood* (1987).

Another great passion is stumpwork from the Stuart era – the use of padded shapes and applied motifs stitched to a ground fabric. Linda likes the profusion of figures, the total disregard for scale

and the lavish decoration.

For future work Linda would like to go much further back into history for inspiration, perhaps to draw from a more primitive and exotic culture such as that of the Incas or the Aztecs.

DESIGN AND TECHNIQUE

Linda's philosophy is to start with the necessity of doing something and then to find a way of doing it. The passion for detail and embroidery was her main preoccupation in her earlier work, and she admits to not considering the overall effect sufficiently. Now she designs with the overall shape in mind, though the work is still made up of small units, which are easier to handle.

Above left Show me thy chink. *1986. 137×91 cm/54×36 in.* ***Above right*** *Detail.*

She begins a new piece by working out the basic outlines. The colours and secondary shapes develop as the work progresses. Sometimes she embroiders directly on to the background. In the picture on page 89, she is working on a cockerel in one of the panels for *1588 and All That*. Linda built up the design with different colours as she worked on the machine. Often, though, she will make up an image and then appliqué it down. She always uses plain fabrics but makes rich brocade-like patterns with her stitching.

The technical breakthrough for Linda came when she discovered she could work the initial stages of the design from the back of the piece. The system she has evolved is to work from an image drawn on Vilene overlaid on to wadding and the base fabric of the panel. Successive layers of coloured fabric are positioned on the front and sewn from the back in straight free stitching along the appropriate drawn lines. In between each stage the excess areas of fabric are cut away from the front. The final embroidery embellishments are stitched on the right side.

The technique is most easily demonstrated by documenting the stages by which *The Pink Lady* was made.

Linda is generous in sharing her skills and knowledge with others. She enjoys taking workshops and considers them an important part of learning. Her attitude is that knowledge belongs to the whole of society and is an accumulation of events and people. She is convinced of the value of acquiring technical skills so that everyone can develop away from simply imitating their tutors. 'Techniques need to be shared: they enable you to develop individual ideas rather than just producing copies. Everyone has a right to artistic expression, and not to be bound by rules.'

FABRICS AND THREADS

Linda lives in Leicester and takes advantage of the many shops that sell fabrics for making saris. One of her favourite fabrics is a silky polyester: she likes the sheen and brilliance of colour, and finds it is good to work with. Its fine weight makes it very suitable for the many layers of appliqué work, although Linda may sandwich muslin between the silk and wadding to give a smoother surface. Occasionally she uses cotton, or velvet as in *1588 and All That*. Recently she has worked with silk and pure silk wadding.

The thread she favours most is 50 embroidery thread DMC or rayon 40 machine embroidery thread – she describes it as 'laying well on the surface'.

Variegated thread with its uneven and mixed colours is useful for depicting details such as hair.

Making *The Pink Lady*

The initial 'sandwich' of three layers was pinned together – the Vilene bearing the drawn outline (it appears in reverse on the back), the wadding and the base fabric (in this case, flesh-coloured beige silk). Using a darning foot, needle size 70, stitch size 0 or drop feed, Linda stitched everything appearing in that colour – the face and features, hands and ruff. Experience and practice have helped her find the easiest routes along the drawn lines. She stitches from the back, but turns to the right side from time to time to check progress. She works mainly with the image straight on, moving it back and forth or from side to side, and avoids swivelling the work around the needle, which causes movement of fabric on the right side.

With the flesh-coloured areas complete, Linda turned the work to the right side and pinned on the next colours – matching the bias and making sure each covered the appropriate part of the design. As dark colours tend to show through lighter ones, the lighter pink came first, followed by the blue. The topmost colour is the first to sew. Working from the back, Linda stitched first around all the areas that were to appear blue, then turned the work to the right side and carefully cut around the stitching line of the blue shapes. She again turned the work to the wrong side and stitched the pink shapes. When she cut away excess pink fabric on the right side, the face and hands were also revealed.

The figure was now complete and ready to be decorated. From this stage on, all the stitching is done from the front, and this is the part Linda relishes most. She uses an ordinary embroidery foot and rayon embroidery thread. By keeping the bottom tension tighter and the top tension looser, she avoids constantly having to change the bobbin thread (this also gives a smoother satin stitch). She began by covering all the raw edges of fabric with satin stitch. When this was complete, she decorated panels of the figure, drawing freehand with the stitching and making up the patterns as she went along, creating texture upon texture to make the scene come alive. Linda has a variety of different stitches to select from on her machine, but frequently uses satin stitch,

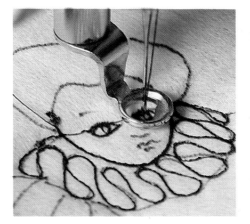

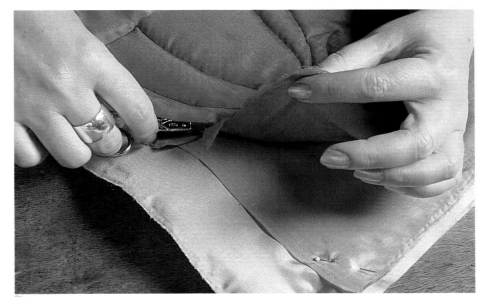

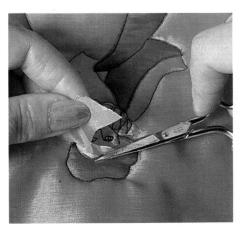

varying the width as the decoration builds up. She feels that a machine with only this stitch available is quite adequate, provided you can manually alter it smoothly while sewing. She finds a hoop restricting, and does not use one.

1588 AND ALL THAT

Over the years Linda has won many awards in recognition of her work and many pieces are in private ownership both in this country and abroad. *Folk Tales* won Best in Show at San Diego International Quilt Symposium, USA, in

1984 and *Under Milk Wood* won Best in Show at the Nostell Priory Great British Quilt Festival in 1987.

Linda's most prestigious to date is *1588 and All That*, which was voted the Champion Quilt in the British National Patchwork Championships in 1988. The theme was Elizabethan England, a period close to Linda's heart, and in celebration of the 400th anniversary of the defeat of the Spanish Armada. Linda knew that this was her opportunity to make something spectacular and she pulled out all the stops in order to achieve it. She felt

Opposite page The Pink Lady *(detail).*
Top *Stitching the details of the face, working on the reverse side.*
Above centre *Cutting out the blue shapes from the right side.*
Above *Cutting away the pink fabric to reveal the face underneath.*

that this piece had to be different from anything she had made before and began by making a list of topics that she felt should be included. A Tudor table-cloth provided the inspiration for the overall design with small panels around the edge. But Linda never begins a new piece by producing a finished drawing to work to. Instead she works out the basic themes and content, shapes and sizes, and then makes decisions regarding the relationship of panels to each other and the balance of shapes and colours as the work progresses.

She chose to work with silky polyester appliquéd and embroidered images applied to a rich, dark blue velvet background. The work took seven months to make and was immediately sold to a private buyer. During the making Linda felt a growing understanding of Elizabeth I and while researching discovered that they had more in common with each other than she originally thought. They are shown together in the top right-hand corner. Linda's current piece is of Romeo and Juliet, set against a Renaissance design.

Through her work and teaching Linda has travelled extensively. She has a special regard for Ireland and France and her greatest enjoyment is to go motor-biking, exploring the countryside, food and wine. As she says, 'Life isn't just about quilts.' □

KEY TO *1588 AND ALL THAT*

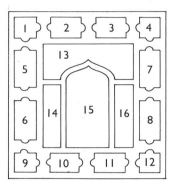

1 The Earl of Essex (in bog) with Tyrone, the Irish leader, in Ireland.
2 Pedlar and bear at the fair.
3 The Americas, and welcome by Indians.
4 Elizabeth I in old age, consoled by Linda Straw.
5 Scenes from rural life.
6 Street scene: dentist, nightwatchman, prostitute, stocks.
7 Shakespeare, the Globe, Titania, Puck, Bottom; Kit Marlowe's murder.
8 Astronomy: Tycho Brahe trying to disprove Copernicus.
9 Mary Queen of Scots embroidering, with executioner in background.
10 Bowls or skittles.
11 Printing.
12 Music and song, with portrait of Catherine Parr and peeper through window.
13 Spanish Armada and English fleet with Philip of Spain.
14 Table with portrait of Anne Boleyn, potatoes, tobacco, the baby James I and VI.
15 Elizabeth I from 'Armada' portrait with Ralegh and Drake.
16 Earl of Leicester, Lord Burghley, Walsingham (with letter), flagship *Ark Royal*. Label on back of quilt: Admiral Lord John Howard (Lord Effingham), Admiral of English Fleet.

Above 1588 and All That. *1988. 244×224 cm/96×88 in.*
Opposite page *Details of top left and bottom left panels.*

STITCHED COLLAGE

'THE WORK I PRODUCE HAS A VARIED NATURE, AND THIS I EMBRACE, FOR I KNOW IT HAS NOT LIMITED AN EXPLORATIVE INTEREST IN MY LARGELY SELF-TAUGHT MEDIUM OF TEXTILES.'

Lucy Goffin

Lucy's pursuits at college took the direction of three-dimensional work. She had originally been interested in sculpture, but chose to study ceramics at Harrow School of Art, preferring the idea of making an object that could be both visually pleasing and functional. It was only when she had finished her course and begun a pottery apprenticeship that she realized that working with cloth held more fascination for her. Stitching and textiles were already an integral part of her life. As a sideline during her student years she had sold Liberty's her dolls and small geometrically shaped fabric boxes which combined her interest in three-dimensional objects with a love of fabric, but it had not occurred to her previously to seek a career in this direction.

She first learned her stitching and embroidery skills by watching her mother sew. Lucy remembers her as a skilful needlewoman who made dresses but also used fabrics and stitching in a very innovative way in still-life collages. Early in her career Lucy worked as an apprentice to a theatrical costumier to teach her more about the construction of clothes and general sewing techniques. 'I was so interested in working with fabric and stitching, and I knew the necessary skill had to be perfected through practice. I wanted my work to be good. If you become passionate about something you find ways of learning about it, you will put time and effort into getting better at doing it.' In recent years she has collaborated with Jean Muir in providing appliquéd decoration for a collection of her jackets.

Lucy made her first quilt when she was at college, drawn to the idea of making something useful from scraps of fabric that would otherwise be wasted. It was also in character to want to make a quilt from fabric she treasured and from bits of material that had warm associations with close family and friends. The first design was based on hexagons, hand-stitched and embroidered. This was followed by another, and again it was on the same principle of using fabrics that were personal – in this case, shirts of the potter who commissioned the quilt.

To date Lucy's career has produced an extremely varied range of work. Quiltmaking has been a constant part of her output, although she has also needed to make smaller, more saleable items such as bags, hats and waistcoats.

Lucy's waistcoats are designed in such a way that they can be either worn (in three dimensions!) or displayed

Above *Lucy Goffin wearing one of her hats.*
Opposite page *Detail of* Dancers.

opened out flat against a wall – like a picture or a Japanese kite.

WAISTCOAT INFLUENCES

The idea of making waistcoats came early on and gave Lucy a free hand to indulge her customers in a wearable item that made them both feel and look good. Lucy's philosophy is that in some way the garment should reflect the wearer, and she has recently completed a waistcoat with the design based on a Mondrian painting for a client who is interested in contemporary furniture and paintings.

It was a waistcoat commission for a painter that led Lucy to develop her present collage technique several years ago. Previously, much of Lucy's work had been geometric in form and character, but somehow that style did not suit the character of her new client, nor was it sympathetic to her interest in painting. Lucy realized she would have to make something very different from anything she had tried before. The

solution evolved while Lucy was discussing the commission: 'We were talking about Harry Thuberon, a painter who also makes partly painted and partly pieced collages from all sorts of things – bits of cardboard, bits of wood. I had recently seen an exhibition of his work and had been very inspired by it. I suddenly thought maybe that this was the direction to develop, with pieces of cloth, so I experimented with little swatches (which is how I start most of my objects). I put pieces together and tried different ways of stitching them, and eventually came to a method that held everything together very successfully but in addition gave another dimension to the finished surface. I did this by positioning my collage pieces and then stitching lines of plain, ordinary machine stitching very, very closely together across the top. I found not only that I had more depth by using different colours in the strips of machine stitching, which gave the collage a sort of three-dimensional quality, but

also that the closeness together of the stitching made the actual fabric itself strong and stable, which meant that I could use free cut shapes, since they were well secured.' Lucy made a simply structured waistcoat and worked the complete surface in the new collage technique. She remembers the event as being 'so exciting and inspiring – I realized it was going to be a very important change of direction.'

As a result, several small collages were made in between her larger commissions. She was all the time considering how to make the collages work together without cancelling one another out. It seemed that the technique needed a stronger framework if it was not to get out of control; this was particularly important on a larger scale, when the collages lost their individual richness if they were placed side by side.

DESIGN INSPIRATION

Lucy has always worked in an intuitive way, an intrinsic part of the design process lying in her response to handling the fabric and experimenting with texture (often made by stitching). She regards drawing as essential to keep her visual awareness sharpened, though her sketches may not lead directly to a specific piece of work. She also takes and collects photographs (such as her study of windows) as an important source of reference material. Her recent design work has developed from either of two approaches. One is visual, based on drawings made in the immediate environment: her studio overlooks Newhaven Harbour. The other is based on imagination, from abstract, intuitive responses in association with dance and music, which are both important elements in her life.

An example of work directly based on drawings made in the vicinity was a recent commission for the Fleetwood Library in Lancashire. Throughout her career Lucy has earned her living mainly through commissions. Her aim was that the wall hanging should reflect the character of Fleetwood, which is a fishing port as well as a resort, and is

Above Dancers. 1985. 61×91 cm/24×36 in.
Left A typical example of the way Lucy groups fabrics at the beginning of a project.

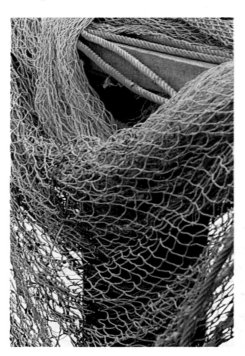

and took photographic references from which she worked directly with the fabrics, first selecting and cutting, then balancing the shapes and colours, with the rhythmic sea swirls, the swaying masts and fishing nets echoed in the linear textures of the stitching.

The vitality of colour, shapes and stitching in the *Dancers* quilt is attributed to music by Mozart, Stravinsky and Ravel, and demonstrates some of the subtleties that Lucy enjoys incorporating in her work. An example is the contrast between the hand stitching, which slightly puckers the red satin fabric on which the light plays, and the hard-edged quality of the machine-stitched blocks that this fabric surrounds.

The *Apertures* quilt which followed was to be on a much larger scale, and once more Lucy was faced with the problem of putting the collages together in such a way as to keep their individuality and 'jewel-like quality'. Again they were strongly linked to the rhythms and colours within music – Mahler, Bartók and Janáček – but now this was combined with the less abstract 'window' idea of looking through, and reflections and shadows.

Lucy had felt in previous pieces – with the exception of *Dancers* – that her work had become too complicated, and in this new quilt simplification was sought. Again she returned to the quilt-making tradition of using repeated blocks, but this time the inner windows were asymmetrical and in themselves created another kind of rhythm across the surface. Her aim was to create a quilt from individual pieces that would also balance in colour and shape in the final piece. It was important for the actual proportion and shape of each colour to link through to give that overall balance. Each collage had a raised piped edge, a three-dimensional touch providing an example of Lucy's meticulous attention to detail.

DESIGN PREPARATION

Lucy allots a good deal of time to planning and preparing her work. She also emphasizes the importance of this early stage when she teaches, describing it as 'a period that helps you to establish the whole thing in your mind's eye, not as a finished thing, but as a spirit that is connected to that piece of work.' Regardless of the project, Lucy has a specific way of working, first doing all her preliminary drawings, designs and note-making in black and white. 'The colour comes with the fabric,' and at that point she will cut out swatches from the fabrics under consideration and put them together in suitable groups which she finds helps to guide her in terms of texture, type, colour and proportion. New inspiration emerges during this selection process: 'The fabrics themselves are very inspirational, and this helps enrich any initial inspiration. You actually build on it by collecting fabrics, cutting pieces out, putting different proportions of colour together – that's very important: the amounts of colour you put together will radically change what you are doing, so in my view it is good to do a lot of that work at the beginning.' At this stage she is also taking into account the practicality of sewing different types of fabric together, considering whether they are compatible in weight and whether perhaps a thinner one will want backing.

As fabrics are selected, so her palette of colour and texture is built up. Although the fundamental idea will not change, it is at this point that alterations may occur in the design. There must be an element of flexibility in order to rethink an idea if it is not working rather than go doggedly on. The preparation time is an opportunity to 'iron out any mistakes – solving them gives you the confidence to go ahead.' It is also when decisions as to detail are evolved. 'I wanted to put some hand embroidery

bounded on three sides by the sea. She was already familiar with the imagery of ports and the medley of fishing boats, nets and so on, but found it essential to visit Fleetwood to make a detailed visual study of the docks and architecture. Her idea was a series of related collages, each one reflecting the character of the area. The overall shape was two connected diamonds, with each one divided into nine smaller framed units. The diamond structure related to other shapes in the building and the framing around each collage gave the observer the idea of viewing a series of different scenes through a window.

Lucy made a number of drawings

Opposite, top left Detail of commission for Fleetwood Library (see Contents pages).
Top right Lucy drawing at Newhaven Harbour.
Opposite left Fishing nets – a typical source of inspiration.
Opposite right Drawing made in the Fleetwood area. 25×30 cm/10×12 in.

in the collar of one of my waistcoats, so I spent quite a lot of time trying out proportions of colour and different stitches until I found something that seemed just right – it went with the stripes of the woven cloth I was using. You spend some hours in preparation, then when you come to construct the piece all those things that have been worked out fall into place, and the overall feeling of the thing is greatly improved.' Once the design is complete, depending upon what she is making, Lucy will then transfer some of the shapes of the drawing on to graph paper so that it will be easier to make the templates. For example, templates were needed for the frames and for trimming the collages to size for the Fleetwood commission.

FABRICS AND TEXTURES

Like most textile artists, Lucy has been collecting fabrics for many years and from different countries. When she begins a new piece she usually first looks to her collection to select fabrics that seem to relate to the project, and then buys to fill in the gaps. The leftovers are then added to her collection so that there is 'a constant feeding into the cupboard, as well as taking out.' Silks and cottons in a variety of weights are favourites.

Many of Lucy's ideas and inspirations have developed through friendships with other artists and craftspeople. This gives opportunities for work collabor-ation and the richness of bringing different skills together. Recently she has used the kumihimo Japanese silk braids made by Catherine Martin. Lucy is particularly interested in using hand-dyed and -printed cloth, and collaborated in a joint exhibition with Susan Bosence, a distinguished hand-block fabric printer/dyer. 'If it was financially practical to work more with hand-made cloth, then I would by preference, because one would feel the quality measured the greater amount of work that goes into the construction of the pieces, and particularly where hand-embroidery or hand-work is used, then the actual quality of the fabric is very important.'

Unless she is limited by the restraints of a commission, texture always plays a strong part in the work – unless it is a piece like the Mondrian waistcoat, which was essentially flat colour. Sometimes the texture is in the fabric, like the black background to the *Apertures* quilt; at other times Lucy will create it with hand or machine work, pleating and tucking, or, in some instances, by making a feature of the way things are joined together. For example, in joining the blocks in the *Apertures* quilt, she double-corded the seams to form a very definite double ridge, giving an important texture when the quilt was side-lit.

DESIGN INFLUENCES

Visits to Japan and, more recently, India have been strong influences in Lucy's career. Aware of a tendency sometimes to over-complicate her work, she feels that the minimal nature of Japanese design is something she needs to make reference to: an instance was with *Apertures* when it seemed essential to bring this 'minimalist' influence to bear. The simple shapes of her garments, and the joining together of the pieces as a whole – together with the surface textural decoration – also show similarities to the Japanese tradition.

More recently Lucy has been designing for a textile and clothing company in Rajasthan, India. The work involves garments and hats as well as quilts, and working as part of a team with tailors, pattern cutters, embroiderers and dyers – a situation she loves and is ideally suited to.

As soon as Lucy arrived in India she realized the country was going to be very important to her, both in terms of the place and people, and because of the fact that textiles are so much part of the daily life. She feels the richness of colour is already influencing her work, and the many fabrics she has brought back will surely mean a change of palette. The impact of a major visit to such a very different culture brings all sorts of inspiration. It is not, however, a question of copying, of reproducing what one has seen: 'That's not what it's about. It's about assimilating experiences and visual stimulus, which then, in its own natural time, will evolve and begin to emerge in the way that one works.' □

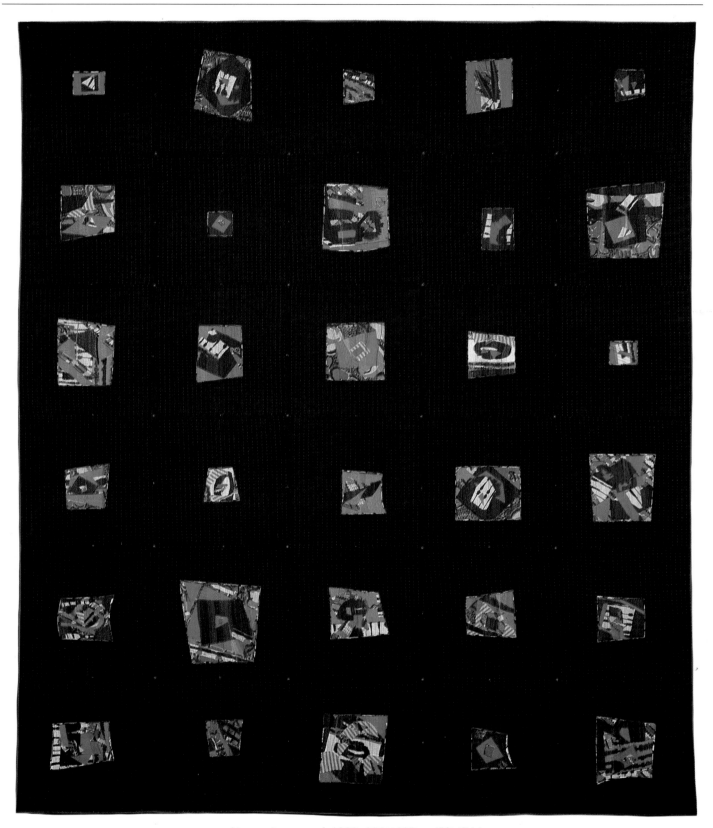

Above Apertures. 1988. 150×180 cm/59×71 in.
Opposite left Folded circular bag, with silk braids made by Catherine Martin. 1988. 28 cm/11 in long.

CHALLENGING FABRICS

'QUILTING GIVES YOU A TACTILE RICHNESS NOT AVAILABLE IN OTHER ART FORMS. IT'S KNOWING THE STRUCTURE AND EVERY INCH OF THE FABRIC, NOT JUST DECORATING THE SURFACE.'

Gillian Horn

As in the classic tradition of quiltmaking, you can read in the mainstream of Gillian Horn's work an integrity that stems from the rhythms of farm and family life. She dovetails the designing, piecing and quilting processes into a busy routine, using, mixing (and often recycling) fabrics that most books tell you to avoid. Her designs, however, are not simply traditional; some are 'borrowed' from another medium, but become hers as she reinterprets a motif and allows the fabrics themselves to shape the design – creating a series of vigorous, strong quilts whose textural interest is as important as their earth-toned colours.

She seems to carry this integrity of attitude through to all aspects of both routine and creative activities. Her 'collections' of sewing materials and artefacts are no museum pieces, but everyday tools that play their own part in the creative process, from the antique treadle machines whose pace she enjoys to the useful Victorian chatelaine she wears on her belt when she takes her quilting outdoors to do in between driving the tractor at harvest time.

INFLUENCES

Although she had once attempted a 'Grandmother's Flower Garden' quilt in which she claims to have made every possible mistake, Gill first became 'hooked' after seeing a patchwork demonstration by someone who was showing the American method of making quilts and using an old Singer sewing machine. To Gill this appeared an ideal combination. She loved the peaceful and controlled way of working, in contrast to the speed with which an electric machine races away with the work, or appears to do so.

Gill consequently attended patchwork and quilting workshops. She had never considered quilting by hand before, but took to it immediately, finding it easy to build up a natural rhythm. The action of stitching seemed therapeutic, and Gill appreciated the textural and tactile qualities it gave the fabric. At the same time she learned to make repeated block designs, but the rigidity of the hard edges and the need for mathematical precision never captured her imagination as quilting had done. She really appreciated the freedom of using larger pieces of fabric, and began to evolve her own style. In the early days she worked only with cottons, but as she became more skilled, she began to work with a wider range of fabrics.

At the same time that she discovered quiltmaking, Gill started collecting sewing machines. When word got around and she found herself deluged with machines, she decided to be selective and to collect only ones made before 1898 (the earliest domestic models became available in the 1850s). She is fascinated by snippets of history such as the fact that sewing machines were the first items to be sold to housewives

__Above__ The chatelaine that Gill wears, lying on a Victorian velvet quilt.
__Opposite page__ Gill Horn in the barn sewing the __Whitney Gray__ quilt; the __Nelson Gray__ quilt is behind.

DESIGN AND FABRICS

Gill's early quilts were traditional designs. She especially admired the rich colour combinations seen in Amish quilts, and quickly learned how colours can change according to the ones they are placed next to. The quilt called *Duo* made in 1983–4 shows how Gill combined a repeated block design with her love for corduroy, velvets and woollen fabrics. She used the reverse appliqué technique to cope with the heavyweight fabrics, and took the opportunity to colour the blocks in as many different ways as possible to break away from the formality of a repeated block pattern.

In Gill's work selecting the fabrics is part of the design process. Gill regards herself as a traditionalist, but actually makes two very different types of quilt designs. Her natural instinct is for earth-tone colours and these she handles most easily and also regards as being very English. She says, 'I don't have to think twice as to whether the colour is right or not – just look at nature.' These are the quilts that she mainly makes as gifts for friends and relations. The second type she finds more of a design challenge. The subjects are various, a response to things that pass through her life. The quilt called *Hidden Alphabet* is typical: it was based on a gothic script and is meant to be an adult's alphabet quilt. The more carefully you look at it, the more the individual letter forms are revealed.

Like most quiltmakers Gill always has several ideas in the back of her mind, and plays with them while she is quilting. 'That's another reason for quilting. While you are stitching, you have time to consider and formulate new ideas – even to discard them, at this stage. It takes as long to create a design as it does to stitch the quilt.'

Unless the fabric is very heavy, Gill regards quilting as the final texturing and delights in creating this by making the lines closely spaced or opened out, and changing the colour of the thread as often as needed. She believes the quilting pattern must relate to or be complementary to the patchwork or ap-

through hire purchase schemes – though it took three male signatures on the agreement form. To date she has some 50 machines, including five treadles and several children's machines and models small enough for dolls' houses. Some of the early ones she bought did not stitch well and ended up as decoration, but others (such as the Whitney treadle on which the quilt called *Whitney Gray* was made) she actually uses for quiltmaking,

preferring the treadle because it leaves both hands free for the work.

She also enjoys collecting and using other pieces of traditional sewing equipment. Her machine collection has led her to collecting wooden cotton reels, old packets of needles and so on – utilitarian, everyday items often with fascinatingly nostalgic fragments of information on their boxes and labels, see pages 138–9.

pliqué – it is not just a matter of following the outlines. Whether patchwork or appliqué, Gill wants her work to retain 'a strong quilt identity' – meaning that it must be made up from three layers in the traditional way.

Although Gill will make a quick design sketch, it is the fabrics and their textures that really fascinate and inspire her to get started. The fabrics dictate the colours, often suggesting ideas of their own that she would never have discovered by just colouring paper. By using the fabrics she already has, she thinks she achieves more exciting combinations than any she might invent. She also visualizes the scale which is dictated largely by the sizes of piece she feels are right for that particular project and tends to work to the dimensions of the fabric, rather than buying a specific length. She particularly likes fabrics with uneven dye or fading, such as you find in old velvet curtains, and is excited by those which already have character. One of Gill's greatest pleasures is going to jumble sales and she tries to fit in as many in one day as possible. Others are looking for clothes and worrying about sizes, but she is just concentrating on the fabric things are made from and is lucky enough to be able to go right in at the end and come back with the greatest treasures. With enthusiasm and confidence Gill uses and mixes 'difficult' fabrics, and this is one reason why her work stands apart from others. As the tactile and textural sides become more and more essential to her work, so she allows herself to be more adventurous. To get the richness of colour that is so important to her she now uses suedes and occasional leather pieces. It is her love of rich textural fabrics, too, that has led her to appliqué much more than to patchwork. Appliqué gives her greater freedom and enables shapes to flow and be less rigid. She likes shapes to be similar but not identical, and finds that patchwork does not offer the same opportunities. 'I like things to be similar

but not the same: I feel they set each other off. It's the same in a quilt – it's more exciting to have similar shapes that blend but are not all stereotypes from exactly the same template.'

Gill is fascinated by all sorts of textiles but kelims are her favourites and have become a recurring theme in her work. *Keshan*, the first quilt based on this tradition, was made in 1985 and won

Opposite page Duo. *1983–4. 135×188 cm/53×74 in.*
Above Hidden Alphabet. *1987. 165×188cm/65×74 in.*

her instant success, being judged best of show at the National Patchwork Championships. The design had developed from a picture of a kelim she had considered for several years as a potential idea for a quilt. She did not use all the patterns shown in the original picture, but selected those that she thought looked most interesting. The blocks are appliquéd and made from velvet and needlecord. Each image has a hand-drawn quality and it is this unevenness which makes the quilt endearing, combined with a rich selection of glowing colours that recall these particular carpets.

In this quilt the placement of the lightest-coloured blocks is especially important: Gill is fully aware of the impact of highlights in a design, saying, 'Everything needs just a little spark to show off all the other colours.' She often agonizes over getting these light-coloured touches in just the right position

but still finds sometimes when put together they become flat and lose the very richness that makes them attractive. Using some pieces wrong side up provides the answer: the subtle difference gives enough contrast to enhance the richness of the other colours. She now finds that qualities of colour and design take over from the technical perfection that many quiltmakers aim for when exhibiting. Gill likes to get her quilts together quickly and makes her work in fairly concentrated bursts before the spontaneity of the idea runs out. The two to three weeks it takes her to actually piece a quilt is the critical time; once the quilt has taken shape, then the quilting can be done at a more leisurely pace. This she regards as the relaxing part. Her timetable is, to a great extent, dictated by the farming routine. She finds the period following Christmas a good time for getting down to her work, when the two boys are fully occupied at school and it is a less hectic time on the farm.

and proportion. When she is really stuck with a design, she takes a black and white photograph of her work: without the confusion of colour it becomes easier to identify and sort out the underlying problems.

She has now been working with velvets and corduroys for many years,

Above left Keshan. 1985. 132×224 cm/52×88 in.
Top and above Gill preparing and tacking the layers together.

Reverse appliqué technique

Like Linda Straw, Gill mainly uses the reverse appliqué technique, working on the wrong side of the fabric and stitching the applied motif before cutting it out. A second line of stitches worked from the right side conceals the raw edges and produces a neat finish. Fabrics that are heavy or difficult to sew need a zigzag stitch first, followed by a satin stitch; on lighter fabrics, the first line of stitching can be made with a running stitch. If the direction of the nap is important – as in much of Gill's work with velvets and needlecords – this needs to be checked.

When Gill worked on the *Keshan* quilt, for example, she would first start by cutting out the required number of squares and marking all the motif outlines on the wrong side of the fabric. She worked each motif individually, cutting the piece of appliqué fabric slightly larger than the size required, then pinning the fabric into position, right side up to the right side of the square. With the work turned to the wrong side, she stitched along the marked outline with a long zigzag through both layers. The work was then turned to the right side and the surplus appliqué fabric was trimmed by cutting it against the outer edge of the zigzag stitches all around the motif. Working on the right side, Gill used a satin stitch to cover the previous zigzag stitching and edges. To do this neatly she always makes sure that the satin stitch is slightly wider than the zigzag.

Gill's method of tacking the layers

Gill tacks her work with the aid of a home-made stretcher, which is like a quilting frame that has webbing attached to all four lengths. She always prepares her quilts in this way and has six battens of 50 × 25mm/2 × 1in wood (two each of 168cm/5ft 6in, 183cm/6ft and 244cm/8ft). These lengths accommodate all her quilt sizes. Each strip is sanded smooth; webbing is attached along one side and marked off in inches. Four straight-backed chairs are also needed to support the wood. Gill overcomes the problems of working on such a large area by setting up the frame outside.

She describes her procedure: 'First position the chairs, then lay the two side lengths across with the webbing uppermost. Add a length with the webbing underneath on top at each end. At each corner where the lengths of wood overlap and meet, the webbing on each should also meet. Clamp the pairs together, first checking the angle with a set square at each corner, as it is essential that the lengths are all accurately set at right angles to each other. When the four lengths have been assembled the inside measurement should represent the final size of quilt plus seam allowances. Mark with a pin the centre point of each length of wood and webbing, and the centre point on each side of the three layers that are to be tacked together. Begin by pinning on the backing fabric first. Pin at each centre point first opposite sides, then opposite ends, then work outwards along each side to the corners. Pin about every 10cm/4in. The tension is less taut than on a quilting frame, but firm enough to keep the layers uniformly tight and together. Make a final check along the edges to make sure that nothing has pulled out of shape.

'When the backing fabric has been pinned on then add the wadding, again lining up the centre points on the wadding with the centre points of the frame and pin in the same way as the backing fabric. Finally put on the top and again pin in the same way.

'The three layers are now ready to tack together. Start tacking from one end that has a length of wood uppermost. Tack rows about every 10cm/4in apart: first one across, parallel to the edge, then others up and down. Complete about four rows of tacking, then undo the two nearest clamps, remove pins, and roll up the tacked area around the wood. Replace the clamps, then continue in this way until the tacking is complete. Throughout the process it is important to keep checking that the

tension is even on all three layers so that one is not pulled tighter then the others.'

RECENT WORK

Two examples of her latest work, *Trio* and *Saddle Ochre*, are again strongly influenced by kelim rugs. Gill finds herself thoroughly fascinated by kelims and the lore behind them, finding 'almost a touch of humour' where the colours change or a design is irregular – 'what many people refer to as the mistakes, where a design has changed or a border does not continue smoothly round a corner.' She tries to incorporate some of these qualities in her work: the subtle fading of her recycled fabrics echoes the variations of the warm earth-tones derived from natural dye-stuffs that grow in the regions where the kelims were woven, and her repeated shapes are slightly varied. 'It's difficult to do this in a gentle fashion, not to have it so obvious that it is called a

mistake.'

Gill admits that this latest work is closely related to the kelim tradition, but feels that she has translated that inspiration, adapted it into fabric, and in the process put something of herself into it. The results communicate the joy and richness Gill gains from the kelims themselves and the shared enthusiasm and pleasure she finds among quilt-makers: she places great emphasis on sheer enjoyment as the main motivation for taking part in creative activities such as quiltmaking.   □

Top Objects collected by Gill, with the quilt Saddle Ochre *and the picture that inspired* Keshan.
Above left Trio. *1988. 137×198 cm/54×78 in.*
Above right Saddle Ochre. *1988. 84×117 cm/33×46 in.*

PAINTING WITH FABRIC

'I WOULD LIKE TO MAKE PEOPLE LOOK AGAIN AT SOMETHING ORDINARY AND SEE THAT IT IS REALLY QUITE BEAUTIFUL IN TERMS OF COLOUR OR SHAPE.'

Jo Budd

Jo Budd studied Fine Art (Painting) at the University of Newcastle-upon-Tyne and it was during this period – she graduated in 1979 – that she first became aware of American traditional patchwork quilts. It was the instinctive use of colour that first caught her attention, and the beautiful effects with which the old fabrics manifested that colour – whereas paint deteriorates with time, Jo noticed how 'fabric seems to gain something as it fades, and becomes more harmonious'. Jo began to work with fabric instead of paint, and found it not only a satisfying medium but one that easily allowed her to manipulate large areas of colour together quickly and positively.

Jo has always approached her work from the stance of a fine artist rather than that of a craftsperson. Colour, light and form are of paramount importance in her work, and there is a constant quest for balance within this framework. Her ideas evolve from an emotional response to the immediate surroundings and can result in abstract or figurative compositions.

Jo's early work was hard-edged, with the fabric stretched taut like a painted

Opposite right *Jo Budd taking a reference photograph.*
Above *Equipment in Jo's studio.*

canvas, and the ideas quite thoroughly worked out before the final piece was begun. Her later work shows a greater freedom in both her design and her working methods, as well as an increased concern with the physical properties of the fabrics.

One concern of Jo's is that today we

are exposed to 'colour pollution' which is as destructive to our senses as that of noise. She fears that our eyes are constantly so overstimulated and bombarded with bright colours that we are in danger of losing the ability to appreciate subtler colour harmonies. One ambition is that her work should make people look again at some perfectly ordinary everyday object – 'a gasometer, a warehouse, or some rusty old corrugated iron shed – and see that it is really quite beautiful in terms of colour or shape.'

A paradox in Jo's openness to inspiration from the purely visual qualities of surroundings is what she calls 'certain barriers which people have with subject matter' – while they can accept stark industrial imagery, a subject like wild flowers may be dismissed as too 'pretty', while something like the deckchairs which are part of her environment have become too clichéd.

'As an artist you have to be very clever to make people see these things with a fresh eye,' Jo says.

COLOUR AND SCALE

Jo considers that her awareness of colour has been heightened by the practice of painting from life, which teaches you to observe and mix colours with acute refinement. Learning about colour, she feels, should come from personal enjoyment and observation – the theory can follow later. Her approach to teaching is to get her students to look closely at some object from nature ('which contains all the most wonderful colour harmonies imaginable'), to observe it properly and then put those colours down on paper. 'From that you build up a sort of library of harmonious chords, and you learn to appreciate the slightly more difficult or "off" colours, where you get interesting, odd combinations.' Jo is always looking out for such offbeat colour combinations – 'It's like looking for new flavours.' She is also fascinated by the way colours appear to alter their hue when used in differing proportions.

When Jo first saw Amish quilts she considered them in terms of the Abstract Expressionists, not as a particular source for her own work – although she uses large areas of colour. The paintings of Mark Rothko have also been a source of inspiration to her, and she feels convinced that artists like him must have been aware of these quilts. She says, 'He totally understood the language to the extent where he has excluded all else, and yet has all the more powerful a message for this simplicity.' Jo, who was classically trained as a violinist, sees parallels between the languages of colour and music, feeling that combinations of colours can be likened to chords in music. When work is progressing well it can be compared with transcendental ex-

perience – one seems to be tapping into something larger than the self, and there are parallels with music. 'The language of music is perhaps more universally understandable on an emotional level, and I believe the same thing exists with the visual arts, except that the language is not perhaps quite as well understood. Colour, light and form are the basis of that language.'

Using colour on a large scale is important to Jo. She feels that with a large-scale picture the viewer is more involved, and actually becomes enveloped in its colour aura, rather than being 'distanced' by a small-scale view. This is particularly true when a large piece is hung in a small room, where one can be aware of all the subtle nuances of colour and texture that take place within a small area of the picture surface – 'compositions within compositions, lots of tiny little parts of a picture which are fascinating to look at. It is equally essential for the work to be powerful from a distance – it should work on another level in terms of the composition, which should balance in some way. Recently the pieces have (I hope) worked in an abstract way from close up, but in quite a figurative way, with almost a three-dimensional feel, from a distance.' The tension between producing a two-dimensional flat object which can

also convey the impression of three-dimensional space is something which Jo feels every artist must be interested in at some time.

PROGRESSION OF WORK

Jo's working and design techniques have changed over the years, in response to her changing subject matter. Her approach started by being faithful to the original shapes of her source material, progressed through a series of abstract pieces mainly concerned with colour, and has recently returned to figuration with a close observation of colour and texture.

In the early 1980s she did her first series of figurative pieces, based on beach huts. The architectural nature of the subject was ideally suited to the simplification of shapes and a straight-edged, formal treatment. One of the major concerns of these works was with the use of clearly defined areas of 'flat' colour to create an illusion of three-dimensional space.

She has always found photography an important medium for recording material and from photographs of the beach huts made small fabric maquettes. These initial drawings were then sized up to full-scale paper patterns so that the fabrics could be cut and sewn together accurately. The large pieces of fabric were seamed from the back so that the picture surface was smooth. The very accuracy of this technique, however, had its drawbacks for Jo, since it did not permit alterations to shapes after the maquette stage, and colour changes were laborious. In the context of later work, Jo sees that the change of scale from small maquette to finished piece also meant that the textural contrasts of the fabrics were diminished.

The piece titled *Gasometer* (1982–3) saw the introduction of raw edges and the use of different textured fab-

rics. In order to achieve this effect, many strips of fabric in graduated hues were sewn closely together, overlapping one another, and with the raw edges visible. She also began dyeing her own fabrics which gave her more col-our subtlety and the freedom to make textural marks. Another innovation was that she began to work directly on the wall, collaging the pieces together *in situ* so that she could see an immediate effect.

The work titled *Scaffolding* was made in 1984. By this time Jo had abandoned any preliminary large-scale drawings and was working directly from her own 'kit' of previously dyed fabrics: 'I would dye up a batch of fabrics beforehand,

Above left Beach Huts. *1981. 183×168 cm/72×66 in.*
Above Scaffolding. *1984. 140×137 cm/55×54 in.*

using procion dyes at this point, making random marks and textures that seemed appropriate, with wax and paste resist methods.' In this case the inspiration was a scaffolded building hung with safety netting which completely obscured the structure itself. 'Sunlight was coming through the netting in shafts, so you had the softness of the netting combined with the structure of the scaffolding poles. These were giving a clue as to perspective, as well as giving a certain depth in space – a fairly minimal depth, because one was looking straight on.' Although Jo used photographs as her starting point, she did not refer to them once she had begun to work with the fabrics, instinctively 'building the thing up, very much like a painting, adding bits or taking them away, purely and simply as to how the thing felt it wanted to grow.' The actual sewing down of the fabrics became a very minimal part of the process, and was relatively speedy once all the pieces were in position. Rather than changing her coloured threads every few inches as the fabric colours changed, she used invisible thread for the first time – 'The stitching was purely and simply a means of holding the fabrics together rather than anything decorative.'

A series based on the surface texture of walls – and in particular those where a succession of posters had been glued on and had then started to peel off – appeared in 1985. Jo began to explore the three-dimensional and textural possibilities of the fabrics themselves, using shadows they could produce. The work had now departed completely in terms of form from its original subject.

'SUFFOLK' SERIES

To date her subject matter had been drawn from man-made objects and materials – albeit ones subjected to natural weathering and decay. In 1986 her own life underwent a change and she moved from an industrial to a rural setting. Three large pieces from this period were based on her perception of the changing colours of the countryside in different seasons – *Suffolk Winter: Snow, Sunlight and Shadows*; *Suffolk Spring* and *Suffolk Summer* – and reflect a softer and more joyful mood, in keeping with the subject matter.

Suffolk Winter was started while Jo was snowed in for three weeks. The fabrics were dyed with a dappled effect using the colour opposites seen in the sunlight and shadows on the snow outside. Sometimes Jo used the reverse of the fabric pieces for its softer marks, giving a water-colour-like effect, which she achieved using new dyeing methods with pigment dyes. The shapes of the large irregular pieces originated in those of the surrounding fields, although this was an instinctive, rather than a conscious, choice. In fact this piece is a conceptual bird's-eye view of the scene. The seamed edges of blocks of fabric appear and disappear as the tonal values modulate across the surface, and some of the seams are sewn from the front to add the emphasis of shadow to an edge. In this piece Jo has moved closer to the quilt form again in its scale (2.4m/8ft square), its loose rectangular geometry, and its derivation from a rural theme – similar to the original American themes such as the 'ploughed furrow' or 'log cabin', for example.

In *Suffolk Spring* the acid greens of the new shoots coming through the snow were introduced to the yellow and blues of *Suffolk Winter*.

The last piece in the series, *Suffolk Summer*, departs slightly from previous working methods and depicts the wild flowers which take over the hedgerows, masking the edges of the fields in summer. The fabrics were all dyed in one session on Midsummer's Day. Jo sponged and painted marks directly on to the white fabric while looking at a bunch of wild flowers. The technique which emerged was that of layering various translucent fabrics which gave veils of colour, like water-colour washes, so that one colour would modulate another underneath. Any marks made

Suffolk Spring. 1986. 183×219 cm/72×86 in.

could also be modified by the fabric on top of them. (This was the beginning of a technique used so successfully in *Dry Dock*.) The new softened approach seemed appropriate for the subject matter, and Jo eventually considered it necessary to sew by hand rather than using the mechanical hard stitched lines of a machine.

'LOWESTOFT' SERIES

A move to Lowestoft in 1987 consolidated this new technique as well as introducing a change in subject matter. Jo's studio overlooks the promenade and the vast expanse of sea and sky. She had to familiarize herself not only with the change of scenery but with a different set of colours – seaside plastics, for instance – and had to learn to work with them in the very different light conditions that prevail by the sea.

She began working on a series of small maquettes of which *Boating Lake* was the most successful. It uses the technique of trapping little pieces of fabric, layered between other fabrics, and then sewing over the top with invisible thread. *Boating Lake* was actually two maquettes which ended up as one. 'The background was produced by sprinkling tiny shards of cut-up hand-painted fabric down on to a canvas layer, and trapping them with a layer of

organdie, which modulated and harmonized the colours of the pieces underneath.' The machine stitching in invisible thread gave a texture without altering the colours: 'I used wavy lines because they were sympathetic to the waves in the sea.' The middle section consisted of a similar process, but had a few brightly coloured triangular shapes on a blue ground. 'I ended up putting the two pieces together without really knowing why, but afterwards I realized it was part of the view from my studio; a boating lake with little toy boats on it, in front of the sea, which I had absorbed subliminally. I realized the background fitted in quite nicely with the wavy lines and the little shapes that could also be reminiscent of fish.' It was the least

and seen from an angle, produce a denser colour than when viewed straight on. The quality of the fabric is thus much more in evidence in that it causes the colours to change as one sees the piece from different perspectives. To Jo this is an important factor in her choice of fabric as a medium rather than paint.

With this technique Jo is both building up and cutting away. The layers are built up with many small pieces, and sometimes she clips down through from one layer to another to reveal a different colour. The final process is sewing the pieces together. With the machine-feed teeth disengaged and using transparent thread, Jo makes 'a kind of scribble with zigzag lines' all over the piece, creating an irregular, slightly quilted effect which unifies the picture

surface and casts subtle shadows.

Dry Dock was made in 1988 and is a powerful rendering of a boat Jo saw being scraped down for repainting. From a distance the bulk of the curved hull gives the work a three-dimensional impact, but close to there is frenzied abstract patterning suggesting the scraped paint: the hull was 'covered in repeated curving marks made when some sort of electric sanding or grinding machine had ground down through various different-coloured layers of paint, which in themselves made marvellous abstract patterns.' To imitate these marks Jo uses a sort of mola technique of sewing through several different-coloured layers of fabric, then clipping down between the stitches to reveal these different layers. She also painted on dyes and in other places

figurative and most instinctive of these small experimental pieces, and probably the most effective.

The next piece Jo produced was called *Red Boat* and was the first in her more figurative current series of work inspired by the massive ocean-going fishing boats. What fascinated her about the boat in question was the textured rusty surface, with bits of red paint showing through in different places. The boat had been scraped in collisions, causing streaks of different colours to mix in with the rust. For Jo this was perfect subject-matter for extending her new technique of using lots of tiny pieces of fabric all collaged together, and for exploiting fabrics such as organdie and muslin which, when dyed

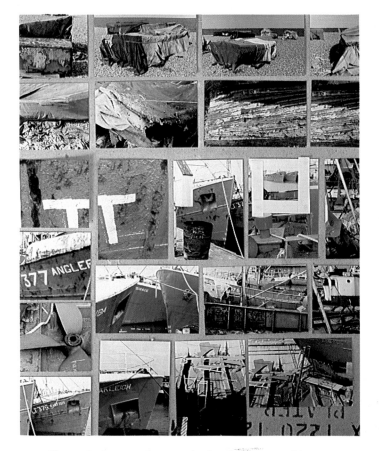

Above *Reference photographs for the 'Lowestoft' series.*
Top left *Collection of fabrics for the 'Lowestoft' series.*
Left *Detail, Boating Lake. 1987.*

collaged back the previously cut-out pieces over other areas of background. In this work Jo has succeeded in capturing the spontaneity of brush marks with the texture and saturated colour of fabric: the term 'painting with fabrics' can truly be applied to her technique.

'I want the piece to read as a complex two-dimensional abstract pattern in the central area, surrounded by slightly calmer, plainer areas of colour,' Jo comments, going on to point out the clues that suggest the form of the boat itself as a three-dimensional object: the curve of the hull, and shadows in the portholes and from the wooden props which hold the boat up. 'I hope the fact that it is a familiar subject matter – although taken out of its usual context – will make the picture's abstract qualities more accessible.'

Jo combines the vision of a painter with the approach of the traditional quiltmakers in the way she believes that things should be made in a craftsman-like manner: 'They must be made with a sensitivity to whatever medium is being used, be it fabric or paint, but must also be robust.' For this reason she avoids using dyes that will fade and fabrics that will rot, and sews everything together in such a way that it can be washed or dry cleaned. 'If you don't enjoy the materials you use, and put them together with love and sympathy and – to a certain extent – knowledge, then the feel of the piece just won't be right.' This acknowledgement of the practicalities of materials and technique is very much part of the tradition. 'Within this premise, I am working towards a greater freedom and speed in the way I work. I believe that mastering a technique or techniques actually sets you free to express yourself better.' □

Dry Dock. 1988. 188×274 cm/74×108 in.

HAND-SEWN PATCHWORK

'I FEEL I CAN GRADUALLY BECOME GOOD FRIENDS WITH FABRIC THROUGH THE SLOW AND STEADY PROCESS OF HAND-SEWING.'

Setsuko Obi

The quilts made by Setsuko Obi illustrate the international appeal of quiltmaking: they combine influences from the very diverse attitudes and cultures of East and West. Setsuko's achievement has been to absorb a design technique that is basically an American invention, and to interpret this with the sensitivity and vision of her own culture – and in Japanese materials – to produce work that is not only personal but unique. In Japan many of the quilts are hand stitched in preference to being machine sewn. In her quiltmaking Setsuko has kept close to her adopted tradition, but achieves a delicate balance by exploring the potential of a repeated surface unit within her own instinctive selection of colours and fabrics. Her asymmetrical use of patterned fabrics softens and dissolves the rigidity of a repeated geometric block to create her own individual statements.

INFLUENCES

Japan has a history of patchwork, largely associated with religion. The Japanese quilting technique, *sashiko*, involves a running stitch used for keeping several layers of fabric together and now employed decoratively, although it was originally applied mainly to work clothing such as that of fishermen, and to firemen's garments, which would have been soaked with water as protection

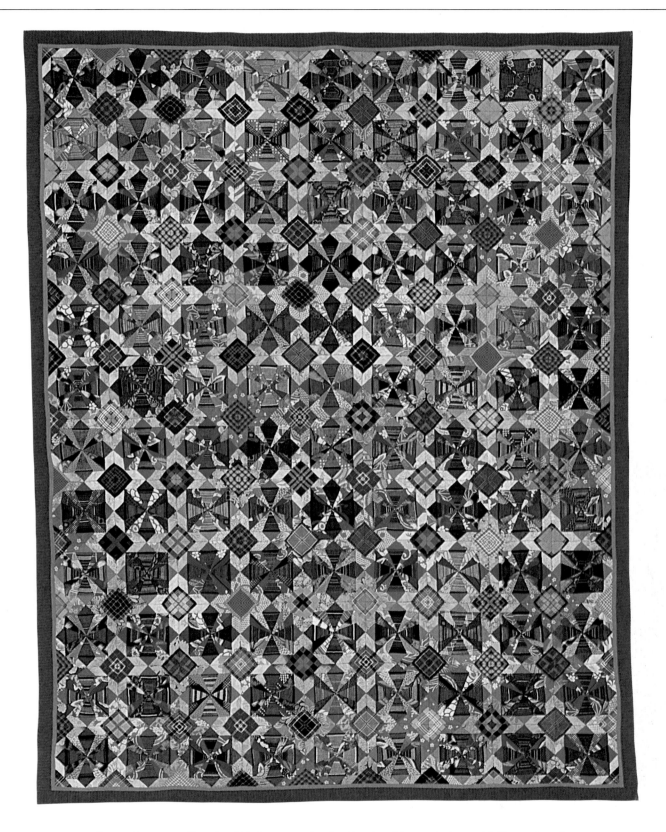

Opposite page *Setsuko Obi demonstrating her hand-quilting technique with* Flowerings I.
Above Flowerings I. *1988. 156×210 cm/61 1/2×83 in.*

before fire fighting.

Quiltmaking has a special appeal to the Japanese, who have a time-honoured respect for the crafts and a strong traditional reverence for textiles. Many old kimonos are painstakingly patched as a way of preserving and extending the life of the garment. Setsuko, like many Japanese women, appreciates the opportunity to work with a treasured collection of fabric and to recycle it into something that will be admired and cherished by future generations: Setsuko intends to hand her exquisite quilts on to her son and his family.

It is possible that Crazy patchwork – which flourished in the West towards the end of the last century – had its origins in the Orient. Enthusiasm for Japanese design in the late nineteenth century made asymmetrical compositions popular in all the arts and crafts, including quiltmaking. Crazy patchwork became fashionable at the time when the Aesthetic Movement was reacting against Victorian overstatement with sparer lines and new asymmetries of design. However, it is the contemporary influence of American quilts and the frequent exchanges and travel between the countries that has brought about the present quiltmaking revival, and which is directly responsible for Setsuko's involvement in designing and making patchwork.

She and her husband at present live in Cheltenham, England. She works on her own, making little contact with other quiltmakers except through such competitions as the National Patchwork Championships, in which her quilts *Flowerings I* and *Flowerings II* were accorded second prize both in 1988 and in 1989.

In Japan Setsuko had taught crafts. She worked in leather and was also a skilful needlewoman: the basic training she received at high school contributed to the high quality of her work. Setsuko's introduction to traditional Western-style patchwork occurred when she and her husband went to live in California in 1977.

Setsuko enrolled in local classes and took up quiltmaking after seeing some work that a neighbour had done. She was immediately fascinated by the craft and began to make quilts and jackets based on traditional block designs and using American fabrics. It was in 1982, after returning to Japan, that she began to draw on her own traditions. She started using Japanese fabrics – and the inspiration they provided – for her quilt designs.

Many of the fabrics she now uses are cut from kimonos that may be between fifty and a hundred years old. She collects these at antique fairs and shops in Japan. She also likes to use the fabrics woven for Japanese blankets (futons) and cushions (zabutons), some of which are *kasuri* cottons with a pattern similar to that of ikat weaving and which may also be made into work clothing. Indigo blue is the predominant colour. The coarser texture of these utility fabrics gives Setsuko's quilts a visual strength that belies the intricate shapes of the complicated block repeats that she so patiently works with. Some of her earlier blocks were quite simple, but later ones – such as those in *Flowerings I* and *II* – are generally more complex, and made from unusually tiny faceted shapes.

All her work is sewn and quilted by hand, and on average she makes one quilt a year. She feels that hand-stitching gives a softer line and finish, and makes the pieces easier to fit together. She comments that the slow and steady process of hand sewing enables her gradually to become 'good friends' with her fabrics.

Setsuko's favourite fabrics are old cottons, linens and muslins. Like Lucinda Gane, she finds that these old materials can be fragile and need careful handling, but that the process of preserving them and giving them new life in quilts is a rewarding one. 'It is a time-consuming pleasure to find fabrics to fit my designs,' she comments.

DESIGN AND TECHNIQUE

Setsuko's designs are based on repeated blocks that she originates herself. She makes a good many sketches and will then select a design or block which she draws out to the finished size on graph card. From this she cuts out the individual shapes which she uses for cutting the actual templates. She makes her templates from thin plastic, as they are used many times and need to keep their shape.

Like Deirdre Amsden, Setsuko plans

Opposite page Flowerings II. *1989. 234×234 cm/92×92 in.*
Above *Block drawn to scale, cut templates and 'taped' patch designs for* Flowerings II.

the colour scheme of a quilt directly from her store of fabrics. Setsuko has devised her own methods of trying out colour combinations by first cutting patches to the finished size and then sellotaping them together from the back to give her some idea of how the made-up design may look. This also gives her the opportunity of combining smaller shapes and enables her to work out the best sequence of sewing the patches together into blocks.

Once she is satisfied with the design and has selected the fabrics, the pieces for the whole quilt are cut out and laid out on the bedroom floor. At this stage Setsuko spends many hours rearranging the patches and meditating upon the design until she feels happy with it. Setsuko considers the placement of colours the most important part of the exercise. She often checks the final design layout by taking a photograph; alternatively, she may look through the 'wrong' end of a pair of binoculars, which acts in the same way as the reducing glass used by Deirdre, making it easier to spot 'mistakes' where the colour sequence does not work or a discordant patch strikes a jarring note. Each patch is then numbered for easy identification and Setsuko sews the quilt pieces into progressively larger units until the top is complete, using the traditional American method of hand-sewing the patches together with small running stitches.

She uses a synthetic wadding and lines it with cotton backing, which is often fabric made for men's kimonos. In preparation for quilting she tacks twice: first the wadding is tacked to the backing fabric, and then these two tacked layers are tacked to the patchwork top. She has abandoned both the hoop and the quilting frame. Instead she quilts with the work draped over her shoulder, as demonstrated in the photograph on page 122. She begins in the centre of the work and gradually works outwards, quilting each side of the patches to give the work solidity. Her stitches are smaller than those seen in British quilting.

Setsuko Obi uses a quilting technique that I first saw demonstrated by Michael James on his visit to England in 1980. A thimble is worn on the middle finger of the sewing hand and another on the first finger of the hand that works underneath the quilt. This thimble has a flattened top and when pushed up into the layers makes a ridge on the surface of the work. The needle guided by the uppermost hand goes in and out of the layers in a straight line that just skims the ridge but makes one stitch. With this method you take only one stitch at a time and pull the thread completely through before slightly moving the thimble along to make the next one.

QUILTS WITH A JAPANESE INFLUENCE

The strength of Setsuko's work derives from several of its aspects. In the first place, the very use of Japanese fabrics is of obvious interest to Western quilters, to whose eyes the unfamiliar indigo-dyed fabrics and *kasuri* weaving combined with unlikely tones have an added fascination and freshness. However, this would be mere novelty if it were not successfully combined with Setsuko's refined handling of pattern and colour. She deliberately breaks the regularity of the block repeat by off-centring any pattern motif within each patch. This skilful manipulation of fabric creates a lively tension, sometimes spinning the shapes and taking the eye right across the quilt's surface, which prevents the repeated unit from becoming boring and static. In her quilt *Flowerings I* the pulsating energy of the fabrics is totally triumphant over the rhythm of the repeated block.

The first quilt she made from old Japanese fabrics, in 1985, is an apparently random placing of many different patterned fabrics. But on further study a desire for balance in terms of pattern and colour becomes evident, as closer inspection reveals the placement of certain patches with large motifs and plain colours which occur as rhythmic repeats to carry the eye across. The design is framed with a bold printed border. This quilt and the one that follows both have an integrity derived from their having been made with predominantly workmanlike materials, including Setsuko's favourite *kasuri* cottons and indigo-dyed fabrics.

Setsuko's second quilt in this new series was made in 1986 and has a more ordered appearance, perhaps in keeping with the minimalism characteristic of Japanese design. It uses two different repeating square-shaped blocks set diagonally on their points. The essence of the design is the fact that two contrasting types of fabric have been used. In one type of block they are lighter-coloured floral prints with the swirl of the pattern breaking the edges of the strips that make up the square. The second block is made from a selection of striped fabrics which, when pieced together, give a concentric framed look to each square. These dark-coloured frames seem to raise the squares off the background to make

an interesting design with a three-dimensional depth. The fabrics are of the type used for Japanese blankets and cushions, and have a fairly coarse texture. The backing fabric is again an indigo material used for men's kimonos.

The quilt titled *Flowerings I* has more of a scrap design character and is busier and more complex than the earlier pieces. It is made from a repeated block in which the fabric patterns in the patches give way to a swirl of colour

and movement in order to lose the identity of their original shapes. Turquoise, acid yellow, lime green and red are vibrating colours against more traditional hues. Checked diamonds attempt to act as regular pinpoints of the design, while floral fabrics spin like windmill blades.

Her latest quilt – *Flowerings II*, which took nine months to complete – uses a more graduated and gentler mix of colours. It returns to using a repeated

block in a straightforward way, but with brilliant manipulation of colour. Tints of varying hues illuminate different areas of the surface, blending subtly into one another across the quilt. The colours seem to drift perfectly naturally through the fabrics as if due to some trick of the light rather than to the painstaking jigsaw-piecing of the quiltmaker. Setsuko Obi's practice of making friends with her fabrics produces exquisite results. ☐

Opposite page *Collection of kimonos and fabric.*
Above *Second quilt made of Japanese fabrics (untitled). 1986. 180×144 cm/71×57 in.*

STRIP PIECING

'NATURAL LANDSCAPE INVOLVES A COLLECTION OF THINGS RANDOM TO THE CASUAL EYE BUT WHICH – BECAUSE OF THE LIGHT IN WHICH THEY ARE BATHED, AND WHERE THEY FALL – FORM PATTERNS.'

Mary Fogg

Mary Fogg regards quiltmaking as an expressive medium in which to convey – in abstract terms – ideas, experiences and emotions which are usually derived from a natural source such as landscape. The strip technique and the vast variety of fabrics used are both hallmarks of her work. One of her strengths is that she chooses not to diversify, as she feels contemporary quiltmakers are often under pressure to do; her continuing involvement with what she calls strip piecing provides ample means for self-expression. Like Deirdre Amsden's pre-occupation with the 'Colourwash' theme, Mary's exploration of the subtleties of 'painting' with strips of fabric leads her to new refinements and depths in her work.

INFLUENCES

Mary attended the Slade School of Fine Art in London during the war years – not a good time for students: galleries had their major works in store and most of the tutors were conscripted to painting camouflage and such like. Since it was the only subject on offer, Mary studied painting, though she would have preferred textiles.

During several years' residence in North America in the late 1950s, Mary had seen many different types of quilt – then less celebrated than they are today

– and enjoyed the juxtaposition of different patterns, colours and textures, with a strong preference for the simplicity of the Amish quilts. But although she appreciated the design element (just as she had been intrigued by the ambiguity of the antique 'Tumbling Blocks' patchwork she had left behind in England, which still had the backing papers intact), the technical side did not inspire her. She admits to being an impatient worker and the idea of cutting out so many pieces and then sewing them together did not appeal. Nor was the technique suitable for the ideas she wanted to convey — somehow she needed to find a broader canvas. A cushion cover was the only result of Mary's early efforts, and she did not take up patchwork again for some years. It was unexpectedly finding the Jonathan Holstein Exhibition of Traditional American Quilts during a visit to Paris in 1972 that really opened her eyes – as it did those of several other quiltmakers mentioned in this book. Mary remembers a hired hand's quilt in particular, with its simple squares of suiting fabrics in subdued colours, and still has a photograph of it in her studio.

STRIP PIECING

Mary began to make quilts seriously in about 1975. Still seeking a non-traditional

A collection of Mary Fogg's quilts.

technique, she had been experimenting with putting together different sorts of fabrics. Finally a solution came from her teenage son's need for a bedcover – something quick to make, economical and robust. She developed a technique using strips of scrap fabric of very different textures that could be sewn together, quilted and backed in one operation. She describes this finished quilt, based on autumn colours, as having 'a ploughed-field effect'. Although it had not been made as quickly as she had hoped, she had developed a technique through which she could integrate many different types of fabric.

Using the strip as the basic unit was the breakthrough Mary had been aiming for. It fitted in with her instinct that stitching should follow the direction of the woven threads, and the 'ploughed' quilting effect created a three-dimensional aspect which held together the different textures. The technique developed for her son's bedcover is basically very simple. Having finalized the design and made the strips, Mary cuts out the backing and wadding slightly larger than the final size and tacks them together. The parallel lines of tacking stitches can also serve as a positioning guide for the strips. Beginning at one edge, Mary lays the first strip, right side up, on the wadding and immediately places the second strip face down on the first; she then pins, tacks and stitches through all the layers along the inner edge of the strips. The second strip is turned over to the right side and opened out, the next placed face down on top of it, and work continues in this way. Thus the strips are sewn together and also to the wadding and backing with only single lines of stitching. Finally Mary trims the quilt to size and binds the edges. Large quilts are heavy to manipulate, so Mary divides them into sections and uses striped backing to hide the hand-finished joins.

In some quilts, however, for example *Thunderbird* and *Desert Landscape II*, the raw edges are deliberately left unfinished, and are fringed. Mary first frays the cut strips slightly ('to learn their character', since different cloths fray differently) and then lays the strips down, each overlapping the one before and leaving one raw edge showing. Since all the strips can be placed in position before being machine-stitched through all layers from the right side, this has virtually turned into an appliqué method. Sometimes Mary couches a woollen thread as she stitches, and depending on the colour of the wool, this either softens or emphasizes the line.

Using an industrial machine

Because of the accurate pinning and tacking involved, Mary finds the sewing process the least enjoyable aspect of her work. She has solved some of the problems of working with large, heavy pieces by using an industrial sewing machine. There are three main types; one with a basic straight stitch, suitable also for quilting; a needlefeed one (the type she has), and an upholsterer's machine. Although an industrial machine is more expensive than a domestic one, there are definite advantages, especially for quilts that are large and thick. The stitching is good and reliable. The foot is heavier and holds the fabrics more firmly, so that the top fabric has less

tendency to pull over the bottom one. The large bed into which the machine is set makes it easier to have the work well supported. The machine stitches much faster, but on most models this is easily controlled.

FABRICS

Mary had to find a sewing technique that would suit her extensive range of fabrics. She regards her work as a 'celebration' of the enormous variety of cloth that is available today. Helping to organize her local Oxfam shop has given her access to all types of fabric that she would otherwise not have seen. She admits to a 'squirrel mentality', collecting and finding it difficult to throw things away, especially fabric. Her quilts include pieces of hand-painted silk velvets, soft furnishing and curtain materials, mixed cottons, tweeds, woollens, silks and corduroys. She says that it is inspiring to see so much material; even in piles on the floor it often suggests new combinations she had never considered. Like Gill Horn, she finds the recycling aspect attractive, and the fact that something has had a history. 'I like the idea that someone in the future looking at my quilts may wonder and think about the fabrics I have put together, and where they came from.'

DESIGN

Mary's training as a painter is an obvious major influence in her attitude towards her work. She sees fabric as bands of colour gradually changing in tones across the surface. Viewed from a distance her work is like a large, abstract painting, with the fabrics integrated to form an expressive and unified surface. It is only on closer inspection that one appreciates the subtlety of stitched lines and textures of woven and printed fabrics. Conveying distance and space is an idea that has always interested her. Generally, she is more excited by the abstract use of colour than the suggestion of form; occasionally work has been initiated by exploring certain colour combinations – *Thunderbird* for example. Her latest 'Desert' series, however, indicates a

new complexity. Her work is usually based on exploring an emotional reaction prompted by a place she has visited and experienced. A stormy Mediterranean seascape, the Australian Red Desert or, closer to home, the surrounding Surrey hills, are all typical examples. The random character of the natural landscape interests her most, and her quilts are a response to the way in which she finds patterns occurring in things 'because of the light in which they are bathed and where they fall.' Although Mary may begin with a definite idea in mind, she also considers working with the texture of fabric is an important part of the process. She believes the 'textile sandwich' of the quilt must have additional texture either in the form of quilting or in the fabrics themselves. The qualities she aims for in her work are tactility intrinsic to the cloth, flexibility so that it can be seen as a three-dimensional object with its appearance varying according to the light source, and the ability to withstand handling. (These points are, of course, in addition to the pure colouring and formal design of the surface which could as easily be rendered by painting as by the qualities of real cloth.) Although she makes wall hangings, Mary places great importance on the movement of quilts and for that reason is especially attracted to making bed covers, which she considers are good sizes for mixed

Above Thunderbird. *1988. 220×185.5 cm/86¹/₂×73 in.*
Opposite page Fabric collages for Thunderbird *showing two colour variations.*

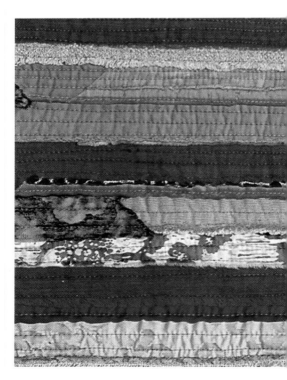

fabric work. She also likes to think of the possibility of her work being made 'just to be dropped around'.

Mary often begins a new quilt on the floor, where she selects fabrics and divides them into tones and colours, which she then regards as her palette. Whatever the design, her method of working follows a similar pattern and usually starts with a photograph or brief sketch. From this she makes small 'fabric sketches', similar to a collage (see the differently coloured ones made for *Thunderbird* on page 131), which she regards as her working drawings and the stage at which her ideas are developed. This gives a much stronger indication than paint of how the design may look, and of the colours and fabrics to be used. From this she progresses to larger fabric samples to try out different fabrics and stitching techniques, before finally embarking on the full-size piece. She composes the design on a large

pinboard before finally sewing the pieces together. The design period is the most challenging and the one she enjoys most. 'It's exciting when the piece begins to show bits of what you had intended, and it's interesting finding out which things work well and which do not,' she says.

'DESERT' SERIES, 1985–7

Mary regarded the series of quilts based on a visit to the Red Centre of Australia as her most ambitious project at the time. It was a 'voyage of discovery' rather than setting out knowing what she was going to do. Before this visit she was already familiar with the country. The idea for the desert series was initiated by a series of photographs taken as she flew over the vast expanse of wilderness and further evolved after the experience of spending ten very hot days near Alice Springs. She arrived back in England with an overwhelming impression of what she wanted to expound in her work: the intense, shimmering dry heat; the great expanse of untamed desert; the emptiness; the extraordinary red sand contrasting with a vivid clear blue sky; the weird abstract rock patterns; a strong ground pattern of scrub and untidy textures; the way that everything that grows just drops and decays. This was no typical desert of golden sands.

Mary started out knowing that she would need to make many experiments and that her work needed to look 'more untidy'. Although she was concentrating on wall-hangings, she wanted the work to retain the feeling that it could be easily handled. After her initial fabric sketches, she experimented with stitching techniques and different fabrics, although she had already decided that the strip was to be the basic unit and vehicle for the overall perspective.

Zigzag stitching and metallic threads were tried but rejected – one for being too regular, the other too obvious. The stitches did pucker the fabric in an interesting way, but over a large area would have been too clumsy. The width and length of strips was a major

consideration: the length had to be sufficient to allow the colour to flow across the surface; shorter lengths gave 'a patchy, brickwall effect'.

Mary places great emphasis on this early stage of experimentation and on constantly questioning what you do and whether it is giving the effect you are aiming to achieve. Finally, she decided on several key factors: to fringe the edges of the strips to give an untidy, ragged effect; to use simple straight stitching which seemed to match the strips best; to decrease the width of strips towards the top of the work to increase the feeling of distance.

In *Desert Landscape II*, the feeling of distance was further emphasized by tonal gradation, the light colours rising with the heat and mountain shapes shimmering and ghostlike in the distance. In strong contrast, the deeper reds and heavily patterned fabric advanced to the foreground and then dropped to the base of the composition. The use of predominantly warm colours emphasized the atmosphere of stifling heat. Slithers of different fabrics were inserted along some strips to break up the continuity and introduce new textures

and colours. Plain fabrics with smoother or no obvious texture were used closer to the top in contrast with large abstract prints and coarsely woven textures towards the bottom. For the first time Mary hinted at possible forms within the composition. The basic strip unit was dissected and new colours inserted to suggest mountain shapes receding into the distance. This further emphasized the feeling of a vast, uninhabited universe. Throughout this design process, simplification was the main factor and is the reason for the success of the finished work.

While she was making the two larger 'Desert' quilts, Mary began collecting fabrics with patterns that suggested aspects of desert landscape. She embarked on a series of smaller studies based on the Red Centre, finding the change in scale refreshing and a good way of formulating more ideas quickly. These smaller works also saw her breaking away from the strips. In *The Olgas*, for example, she has incorporated larger areas of fabric within the strip tradition. The bold abstract shapes in the red fabric suggested her feelings about that area. She also purchased the

Above *Objects collected by Mary on her Australian trip.*
Top left Desert Landscape II. *1987. 183×118 cm/72×46½ in.*
Left *Detail,* Desert Landscape II.

material in different colourways, and used these in the foreground.

Using photographic reference the design was gradually built up, starting with the main central shape and then working towards the foreground. For the sky, she recalled the intense blue, gradually darkening it towards the top for maximum effect. Again, Mary worked on the floor for the initial idea, but later transferred the fabrics to a piece of cork covered with an old blanket. All the pieces were first pinned in position then eventually tacked to the blanket and backing fabric before being stitched down, the lines of stitching making an important contribution to the overall texture and getting progressively closer towards the top of the work.

RECENT WORK

In working to commission Mary enjoys the challenge of 'exploring an idea you may not have considered for yourself'. In fact, it was producing work to order that made her realize how important it is to produce a 'mock-up' – both for her own use and to discuss possible ideas with the client. Recently she completed a large curtain to hang over the west door of a church, and emphasizes the need to take the fabrics under consideration to the building itself, to see how they react with the surroundings, the light patterns and the architecture. In this case the colours were dictated by the stained glass window immediately above, and many were specially dyed; the textures – fringed woollens – were suggested by the scale and materials of a medieval church, and the forms echoed the gothic architecture. The design of this piece was planned so that a dozen church members could help in the making up.

Mary has continued to explore the possibilities of overlapping strips of fringed woollen cloth. One recent quilt depicts a formalized waterfall in the colours and tones of North Wales. □

Top The Olgas. *1988. 36×47 cm/14¼×18½ in.*
Above left One of Mary's photographs of the Olgas. *Above right* Working stage of The Olgas: strips pinned to cork board.
Opposite page Mary working out a design for The Olgas.

CHAPTER 3

QUILTMAKING TECHNIQUES

This section is aimed at giving the basic skills required for quiltmaking. Many of the techniques are based on my own experience as both designer and quiltmaker as well as on that of other quiltmakers featured in the book. These pages do not set out to describe every quiltmaking technique available, but rather to guide newcomers who have read the book and would like to get started on their own quilts. Terms mentioned earlier are also explained more fully here.

Each quiltmaker whose work has been shown has her own repertoire of skills which have been developed and adapted to her own requirements (for example, Linda Straw on page 92 shows how she uses the machine appliqué technique that is done on the reverse of the work), but here I describe the more basic methods. The techniques do not have to be rigidly adhered to and I suggest that you explore several methods experimenting with both hand and machine work to find the ones that suit you best.

In this chapter we are describing a quilt in the traditional sense, the top being patchwork, appliqué or plain, and the three layers held together with quilting stitches. This chapter runs in the same sequence as one would make a quilt, beginning with choosing fabrics and making templates. Patchwork techniques follow, including information on Seminole work which is featured in Eiluned Edwards' new work. For those who prefer to sew patchwork by hand using the backing paper method, see page 68. Appliqué comes next; this is a technique that offers possibilities for illustrative work and can be combined with patchwork or made on its own. Quilting both by hand and by machine completes the chapter. I have concentrated on using a hoop for the hand-quilting technique since during my research I found this to be a much more popular method and most likely to appeal to beginners.

The basic skills discussed on the following pages are easy to master and provide a useful starting point for further exploration.   □

Detail of reverse side of Checkerboard Squares. *Deirdre Amsden. (See page 51)*

PATCHWORK

SEWING MATERIALS AND EQUIPMENT

Most of the equipment used for patchwork, appliqué and quilting you will probably already have for general sewing. If not, invest in the best equipment you can afford as it is false economy to buy cheaper versions that do not last so well. Efficient equipment is much more enjoyable to work with and helps towards achieving a professional finish. The basics are:

Fabric cutting shears They must cut through several layers at once.

Small pair of scissors For trimming ends etc.

Rotary cutter Also for cutting layers of fabric (optional).

Needles Sharps 8–9 and a selection of hand-sewing needles.

Pins I find that glass-headed pins are some-times too clumsy for finer work, so aim to keep a selection which includes lace pins.

Thimble (for hand sewing) It should fit comfortably on the second finger of your sewing hand.

Metre rule For measuring and drawing straight lines.

A set square is also useful for right angles.

Dressmaker's ruler This is one of the most useful measuring devices to have. It is a transparent ruler marked with a square grid and very good for marking seam allowances.

Coloured pencils For marking fabric and designing.

Sewing machine This depends on your own preference for hand- or machine-stitching. One that works satin stitch is useful for appliqué.

Iron I use a steam iron with a pressing cloth to prevent glazing the fabrics (especially black cotton), but several quiltmakers found a steam iron too heavy and preferred a dry iron plus water spray gun.

Seam ripper Jean Sheers commented that this was her most useful piece of equipment! Essential for unpicking machine stitches.

Fabric The previous chapter demonstrates that almost any fabric can be used or adapted for quiltmaking. I began making quilts using cotton fabrics and still use them; not only are they easiest to handle, but they are available in such an extensive range of colours and patterns. Specialist mail-order companies offer the best selection and will send samples on request (see page 156). The availability of fabrics in shops is dictated by the whim of fashion, so my advice is to buy a fabric when you see something that you like and build up your own collection. Store on cardboard rolls if possible to keep free from creases.

Your method of sewing should also be considered when selecting fabrics. Dress-weight pure cotton is ideal for either hand or machine work, but some heavier fabrics are better stitched with a machine. If the quilt is to be laundered, wash all the fabrics before using to test for colour fastness and shrinking. Make sure you have a wide range of tones, colours and different types of print – variety seems more important than quantity. The fascination of traditional quilts is often the fact that the colours vary even if it was intended for them to be the same. In the past many quilts grew out of a scrap bag, but today there is a stronger tendency to go and buy specific material for a project. This does not necessarily guarantee success.

The selection of fabrics, as in Setsuko Obi's work, plays a significant role in the appeal of quilts. I find the anonymity of spots, stripes, checks and plain fabrics more appealing than many of the floral patterns, unless their identity is skilfully submerged as in Deirdre Amsden's 'Colourwash' series. The texture of printed fabrics can be an important element within the design – in fact, it can be the initiating factor. Mary Fogg's *The Olgas* originated when she found fabric that suggested to her aspects of desert landscape (see pages 132–4).

Threads It is not necessary to change the colour of thread for different fabrics: instead, select a neutral colour such as grey or beige that can be used throughout. For hand-sewing use a No 50 cotton or special quilting thread. Run it through beeswax to help it glide through the fabric and knot the end that you cut to prevent twisting. For machine-sewing, match the thread to suit the fabric.

Templates Templates are the master shapes from which all the patches are cut and must be accurate for the pieces to fit together. You can either buy templates or make your own, which is cheaper and more flexible.

EQUIPMENT FOR MAKING TEMPLATES AND DESIGNING

Most of the equipment needed for making templates will also be useful for designing and can be purchased from art shops.

Graph paper (square and isometric) Most template shapes can be cut from these grids. Choose either imperial or metric.

Tracing paper For drawing designs.

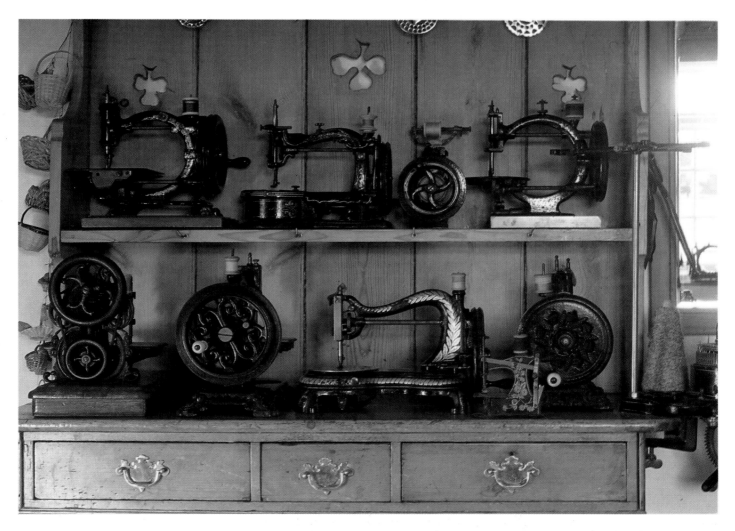

Metal ruler Both for measuring and for cutting against; more accurate and safer than a plastic ruler.

Scalpel or craft knife with replaceable blades For cutting templates.

Cutting mat Provides an indestructible surface for cutting out templates etc.

HB and 2H lead pencils and/or fine black felt tip pen.

Coloured felt tip pens For design work, not marking fabric.

Card The thickness depends on how many times the shape will be used, but it must be firm enough to be drawn around easily without bending. Setsuko Obi uses thin plastic, which keeps the shape well and is good for small patches.

Paper-cutting scissors.

Spray adhesive One has recently been marketed which is free from chlorofluoro-carbons. Glue sticks are an alternative, but make sure the paper does not get too wet.

Objects from Gill Horn's collection: **Top left** *Cotton reels.*
Top right *Antique sewing machines.*
Above *Packets of sewing needles.*

HOW TO BEGIN

In order to illustrate various techniques I have chosen as an example a small quilt made by Gill Horn and four of her friends several years ago. Through making this piece they exchanged ideas about design and acquired basic knowledge and quiltmaking skills. Each made several blocks which she signed, then they shared the work of sewing them together and finally of quilting. At the end of the project they drew lots to determine who kept the quilt, and Gill Horn was the lucky winner. The design

MAPLE LEAF BLOCK

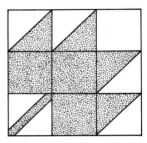

shows a repeated block called 'Maple Leaf'. The quilt was made from scraps of fabric and the colours based on those of autumn.

Using a repeated block pattern is a good way to start. It is a traditional method of making a quilt design, but one that has enormous potential for individual interpretation. For example, throughout most of her career Pauline Burbidge has been exploring repeated block designs.

A block is usually square, and made from a number of different-shaped patches that work together to make a pattern. It can be patchwork (as in this case), appliqué or quilted, or may contain elements of all three. When the blocks are repeated, larger overall designs are made which were not conceivable by looking at an individual unit. It is said that the idea of making quilts in this way developed from the early American pioneers who lived in such cramped conditions that working on a large bed-size quilt would have been impossible. Working on smaller units that were joined together during the last stage provided a more flexible alternative.

Making a design

A design is needed to plan out the pattern, colours and size. It is also a useful guide when making up the quilt.

One of the most straightforward ways to

MAKING A REPEATED BLOCK DESIGN

make a design is to draw one block to a reduced size on graph paper, then to place a sheet of tracing paper over the top and with a lead pencil or fine black felt-tip pen trace it off a number of times. Either place the blocks side by side, or experiment with the placing – as in this quilt, for example, where four blocks are set diagonally to make a different central pattern. Borders are useful to frame the quilt and make it up to the required size. You can draw directly on the graph paper but using tracing paper allows greater flexibility to experiment with the position of the blocks and also gives you a line drawing that can be photocopied. Make several copies to work out the colours that you want to use and templates required. If you do not have access to a photocopier, apply colours to a tracing paper overlay.

Once you are satisfied with the design and have decided on the colours, it is necessary to finalize the size of the quilt before making the templates or calculating fabric amounts. It is useful and sometimes easier to draw up the block or part of the design on graph paper to the finished size. This can also be referred to for the template sizes. Make sure the patches are a

comfortable size to sew and note how many templates are needed. In this quilt, for example, each block measured 16.5cm/6½in square and from this the other shapes and border were easily calculated.

Making templates

Draw out each shape on graph paper with a 2H lead pencil. If the patchwork is **sewn by hand** the template is made the same size as the finished patch. Add a 6mm/¼in seam allowance to each edge if **sewing with a machine**. Stick the graph paper on to card and cut around the outside edge.

THE SIX TEMPLATES NEEDED FOR THE *MAPLE LEAF* QUILT OPPOSITE

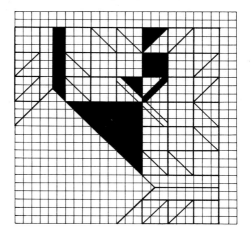

TEMPLATE FOR HAND-SEWING

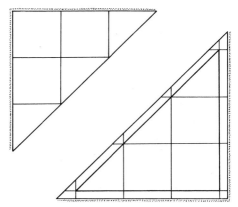

TEMPLATE FOR MACHINE-SEWING

Estimating fabric

Fabric amounts can be estimated once the templates are made. Refer back to your original design and count how many patches need to be cut from each template and in which colour. Make a note of this on each template as a reminder.

To estimate for one colour, take a length of 90cm/36in fabric (or a ruler that length) and see how many times the template will fit from selvedge to selvedge. Remember to include seam allowances if they are not on the templates. Divide the total by this number, then multiply by the width of the template. Also use the width of the fabric for calculating borders etc. For different fabric widths, adjust these calculations accordingly. When you place a template on the fabric try to align the longest edge either with the straight grain (selvedge) or the cross grain. Avoid the diagonal bias.

Marking and cutting the fabric

Always mark out the patches on the reverse of the fabric with the template wrong side up. This is important when using non-reversible shapes. I find it easiest to begin by marking a line parallel to the straight grain edge about 12mm/½in from the edge and placing the templates on it.

For **hand sewing** draw around the template, then add the seam allowance to each edge. Place the next shape a seam allowance away from the previous one and continue in this way. The inside line is for stitching while the outer line is for cutting.

For **machine sewing** butt the shapes together and mark around the outside edge of the template, which is the cutting line. With either method aim to line up the patches and marked lines if possible, because this makes it much easier when cutting out the shapes.

MARKING AND CUTTING (hand-sewing)　　**MARKING AND CUTTING (machine-sewing)**

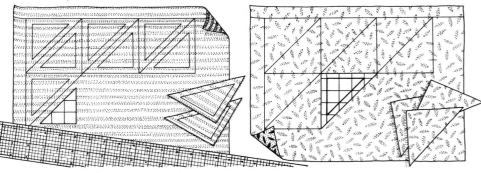

Opposite page Maple Leaf *quilt. 89×89 cm/35×35 in. Jackie Chalcroft, Gill Horn, Gillian Horn, Ann Newberry, Denise Orange.*
Above *Mosaic patchwork quilt (detail). Welsh. Victorian. Silks.*

Sewing sequence

When the patches are cut, consider next the most straightforward way of sewing them together (this applies to both hand and machine work). The main principle is to sew into progressively larger units until the work is complete. For example, in the 'Maple Leaf' block the triangles are sewn into squares, these are sewn into rows, and the rows are sewn together to make blocks. If the quilt is made from repeated blocks, the blocks are sewn into rows and then the rows are joined to complete the design. In the 'Maple Leaf' quilt shown here, the basic blocks are joined together with other linking shapes into five main sections, which are finally sewn together to make up the complete design.

SEWING PATCHES TOGETHER

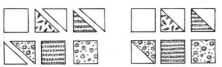

MAKING A DIAMOND PATTERN

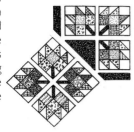

HAND-SEWING PATCHWORK

This is the way Setsuko Obi makes her quilts. Since it is also how the traditional American quilts were sewn, this technique is often referred to as 'the American method'. The patches are sewn together with a small running stitch following the pencil line on the back of each patch.

Sewing the patches together

Place two corresponding patches right sides together and pin so that the pencilled lines on both patches are aligned. Insert pins at right angles to the sewing line so that they are easier to remove. Do not sew through the seam allowance but begin stitching at one corner and proceed to the next, removing the pins as you go. Start with a knot and end the sewing with several backstitches. While sewing, check the back of the work to make sure you are stitching along the pencil line on both sides. When all the patches are joined into rows, then sew these together. Take the first two rows, place right sides together and pin. Pin at each end of the row and where seams meet, then place extra pins in between. Again stitch together by sewing along the pencilled lines and avoiding the seams. Continue to join all the rows together until the work is completed.

Pressing

Leave pressing the patchwork until the end so that the seams are not stitched through. The seams are stronger if pressed to one side, usually towards the darker fabric. Alternatively, press all in the same direction.

First iron the back of the work, then press the front lightly so that the fabrics are not completely flattened and lifeless.

Whether you use a dry or steam iron, cover the patchwork with a pressing cloth to avoid glazing the fabrics.

PRESSING THE BLOCK

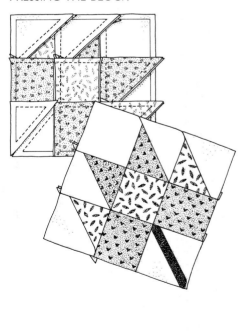

SEWING PATCHES TOGETHER

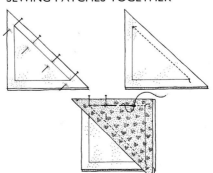

SEWING ROWS TOGETHER

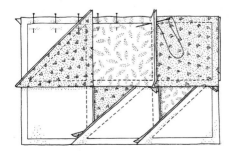

Opposite page Setsuko Obi's first quilt using Japanese fabrics (untitled). 1985. 163×204 cm/64×80 cm.

MACHINE-SEWING PATCHWORK

Whether you stitch by hand or by machine is a matter of personal preference. A popular method is to make the patchwork by machine and then to do the quilting by hand. This is the way Deirdre Amsden chooses to make her quilts.

The technique of machine patchwork is dependent on the edge of the patches lining up with the edge of the presser foot. On most machines this gives a 6mm/¼in seam allowance. (Occasionally it is 9mm/⅜in, and the templates need to be adjusted.) Some machines (like the one Deirdre uses) need a strip of masking tape to be placed on the plate 6mm/¼in from the needle, and the patches are aligned against that.

As the patchwork is sewn the seams are pressed open, so have an iron nearby.

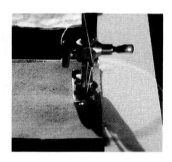

Sewing the patches together

Using a stitch length to suit the fabric, place two patches right sides together and pin. Again keep pins at right angles to the line of stitching for easier removal, and remove each before it goes under the presser foot. Start stitching a little way in from the end then reverse back to secure the stitches before working to the other end, securing with several backstitches.

Identical pairs of patches can be sewn with continuous thread. Feed the pinned patches through the machine, sewing as described. At the end of each pair, raise the needle and presser foot, pull the threads slightly before dropping the foot again and commencing to sew the next pair. Continue until you have a chain of patches that can then be separated and trimmed.

Always press seams open before joining units together. Pin at each end, then at matching seams, and in between as necessary. Again stitch with the edge of the patches aligning with the edge of the presser foot to keep the seam allowance constant throughout. On completion, press all seams open on the back, then turn to right side and gently press the front.

SEWING PATCHES TOGETHER

FINISHED BLOCK

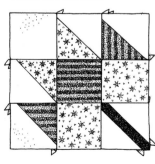

SEWING ROWS TOGETHER

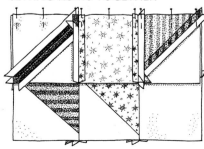

Above left Aligning patches against masking tape on the sewing machine's plate.
Above Deirdre Amsden sewing a chain of patches.
Opposite page Detail, MRI. Eiluned Edwards. (See pages 44–5)

SEMINOLE PATCHWORK

Seminole patchwork, developed by the Seminole Indians of Florida, was originally used to decorate clothing but is now frequently adapted to quiltmaking. Eiluned Edwards uses it in her *MR1* (see page 44). The Seminole technique is quick to do and permits more intricate patchwork designs on a smaller scale than one would normally work using the conventional patchwork methods. You can make a complete quilt using the Seminole technique or insert small areas, as Eiluned has done. Although the work appears time-consuming and complex, the making up is in fact very easy and quick using a sewing machine. Endless variations are possible. Basically, strips of fabric are sewn together, then cut and repositioned to make new designs. Reversing contrasting strips makes a chequer pattern. Staggering the strips and then cutting them diagonally makes a diamond pattern. Dressweight pure cotton fabrics are recommended, usually in plain colours to show the effect more clearly. It is best to start by making up samples and exploring what the technique has to offer. Remember to allow for seam allowances when cutting and make these strips wider.

CHEQUERBOARD PATTERN

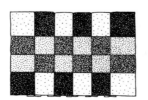

DIAMOND PATTERN

APPLIQUE

Appliqué, like patchwork, can be sewn by hand or by machine and in several different ways. The fact that you are laying one fabric over another — rather than fitting pieces together like a jigsaw puzzle, as in patchwork — makes it a more flexible technique.

Different examples of appliqué seen in the previous chapter include the work of Gill Horn (see page 104) and Linda Straw (see page 88), both of whom work from the back of the work rather than the front, as in the technique shown here..

The fabrics and equipment are similar to those used for patchwork, but appliqué also gives the opportunity to use heavier fabrics and mix different weights within one quilt.

HAND-SEWING APPLIQUE

Both Liz Bruce and Janet Bolton sew appliqué by hand with the raw edges turned under, but each has very different ideas on stitching and the part it plays in the overall design. Janet considers hers part of the visual 'show', but Liz's stitches remain almost invisible, as described in the technique opposite.

Hand-stitched appliqué quilt (detail). Welsh. 1930s. Cotton.

Making templates

Unless you intend to work in a way similar to Janet Bolton's (see page 54) and to cut directly into the fabric, templates will be needed for each individual shape in the design. The most straightforward way of doing this is to make a full-size drawing on tracing paper, then trace down each shape on to thin card and cut out. Seam allowances are always added to the fabric rather than the template for both hand- and machine-sewing. Number each shape on both the drawing and the template for easy identification on complex designs.

MAKING TEMPLATES

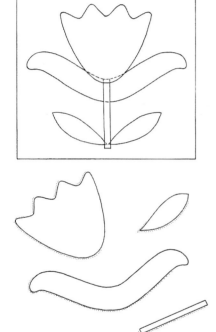

Marking and cutting the fabric

Place the template right side up on the right side of the fabric. Mark around the edge with a coloured pencil (this will be the folded edge) then add a 6mm/¼in seam allowance. As for patchwork, try and place the template on the straight or cross grain of the fabric. Roughly cut out the shape so that it is easier to handle while staystitching. **Staystitching** is not essential, but it helps to make the folded edge easier to turn under neatly. Either machine- or hand-stitch just outside the marked line which is to be folded back.

Cut out the shape around the outer marked line. Clip curved edges so that they lie flatter when turned under.

MARKING FABRIC

STAY-STITCHING

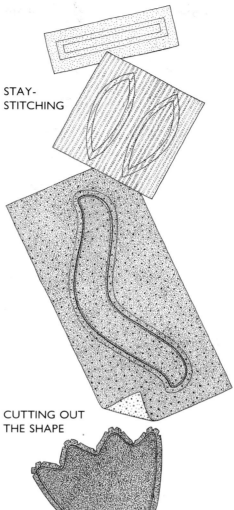

CUTTING OUT THE SHAPE

Tacking

Working with the right side of the shape uppermost, gradually fold back the seam allowance, following the marked pencil-line so that the staystitching is hidden on the back. Aim to keep curved edges as smooth as possible. Tack the edges down to keep in place while stitching.

TACKING THE EDGES UNDER

Stitching

Before stitching work out how the shapes will fit together — for example, tuck flower stems beneath the leaves. Place the shape in position on the backing fabric. Pin and/or then tack down. Sew around the appliquéd shape with a small, neat overcast stitch to the background fabric. Remove tacking and lightly press.

STITCHING TO THE GROUND FABRIC

Finishing

To complete the appliqué the backing fabric behind the shape can be removed. This reduces the thickness of layers if the work is to be hand quilted, helps the shape to lie flat and stops the background fabric showing through if it is darker than the top. Turn work to back and with a small pair of scissors carefully cut away the background fabric 6mm/¼in inside the line of appliqué stitches. Gently press both sides.

FINISHING   wrong side

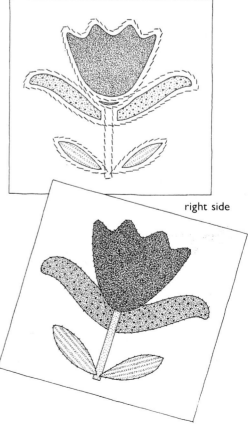

right side

147

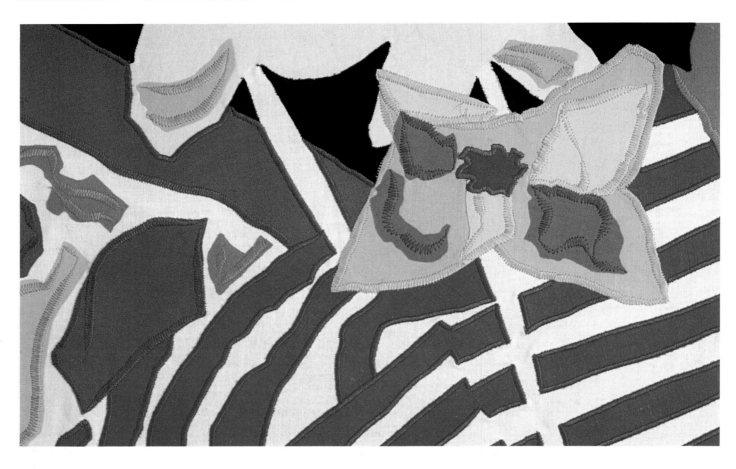

MACHINE-SEWING APPLIQUE

A desire to work more spontaneously with fabric is the main reason why an increasing number of quiltmakers and textile artists are working with machine appliqué. For Jo Budd, Pauline Burbidge and Lucy Goffin the concern for turning under and concealing raw edges is no longer a major priority. In fact, inherent 'problems' such as fraying edges are now being explored for their expressive possibilities. Machine appliqué is not a substitute for hand work but offers a completely different range of effects, such as the stitched collages by Lucy Goffin in her quilt *Apertures* (page 103) or the slithers of fabric trapped under a transparent layer and stitched down in Jo Budd's *Boating Lake* (page 118). Pauline Burbidge has a new-found freedom through using Vilene Bond-aweb, a fusible web that bonds one fabric to another. The technique is both easy and quick to use and gives the surface of the fabric a smooth, flat appearance. The web both is machine-washable and can be dry-cleaned. It is not, of course, essential to use a fusible web for machine appliqué. The shapes can be easily cut out to the finished size, pinned and tacked or stitched to the ground, and the raw edges covered with a machine satin stitch. Fusible web can also be used with hand sewing.

Using a fusible web

A fusible web enables appliqué shapes to be ironed on to the background, and stitched around after if desired. The web is covered on one side with paper.

Take a piece of web and place adhesive side down on the wrong side of the fabric. With a medium-hot dry iron, iron over the paper side to bond it to the fabric. Either use a template or draw directly on the paper, reversing the image.

Cut out the shape then peel off the paper. Position the image on to the background fabric, then iron over with a hot dry iron, preferably using a damp cloth. Leave to cool before doing any further work. Either leave the edges raw or stitch over.

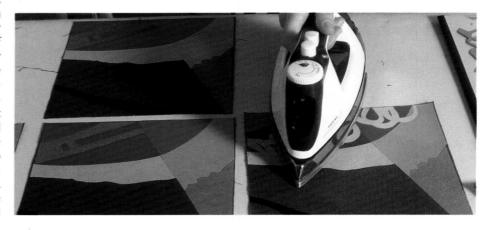

BORDERS AND BACKING

It is a common practice to add a border to a patchwork or appliqué top. This serves to frame the design and is a useful way of making the work up to the required size, if necessary. Sew by hand or by machine.

Making a border

Refer back to your original design for the size of the border. Cut two pieces of fabric to the length of the top plus seam allowances, and two pieces to the width of the top plus the borders and seam allowances. Sew the borders to the main piece in the same sequence, first to the sides and then to the top and bottom.

ADDING THE BORDERS

Making a backing

If the work is to remain unquilted (like Lucinda Gane's, for example), then it requires a backing. This can be made in several ways. Unbleached calico is an ideal fabric, but wash before using. The edges, although unquilted, can be self-bound (see page 155). Alternatively, cut the backing to the same size as the top, including seam allowances. Place the top and backing right sides together, pin, then machine stitch around all edges, but leaving the centre third of the last edge open. Use this opening to turn the work to the right side, then close the gap by slipstitching by hand.

Keeping the layers together

To stop the two layers from shifting apart either tie together, using a thick cotton thread and making a small reef knot (right over left, left over right). Or make a cross stitch, then cover with a small bead or button. Repeat about every 150mm/6in.

Opposite page, top *Fabric collage sample for* Shipshape. *Pauline Burbidge.*
Left and above *Pauline Burbidge working on* Shipshape *in her studio.*

QUILTING

HAND-QUILTING

Quilting gives texture to a plain surface, can emphasize shapes or be used to blend fabrics together, as seen in Deirdre Amsden's work. The quilting stitch serves two purposes – decoration, and the function of holding the three layers together. Quilting can be hand- or machine-stitched, each option creating a very different character. For hand-quilting I strongly advise you to use a hoop to keep the layers together and evenly stretched. Although Setsuko Obi quilts without hoop or frame, this does seem to be an unusual exception. Fewer quilters use a frame today, although they are available from specialist suppliers and some people make their own. A hoop has several advantages: it makes the work easily portable, you can stitch in any direction, and you can easily manoeuvre the work to take advantage of the best available light. Many quiltmakers look on the time they spend hand-quilting as giving them the opportunity to contemplate and plan their next work.

SEWING MATERIALS AND EQUIPMENT

Some of this has already been mentioned, but there are a few extra items:

Quilting hoop Similar in principle to an embroidery hoop. Sizes vary, but buy a fairly large one (45–56cm/18–22in diameter).

Thimble You will need two, one with a flattened top if you are using the method described by Setsuko Obi on page 126.

Needles Use Betweens 8–9.

Fabric The top and backing fabrics should be of similar weights and pre-washed to remove any dressing and to test for shrinkage, colour fastness etc. Cotton sateen was an old favourite for plain quilts because the slight lustre of the surface showed off the quilting so well, but is no longer available. Natural fibres (pure cotton or cotton/wool mix) are popular as they are easy to quilt. Quilting patterns show up better on lighter-coloured plain surfaces and the lustrous fabrics such as polished cotton, satin and silk further enhance the 'sculpted' quality of the work. If you are concerned about the unevenness of your stitches on the back, choose a patterned fabric instead of plain.

Above *Detail of Northumbrian quilting.*
Opposite page *Typical backing fabrics found on Welsh quilts*

Wadding or filling A wadding is the centre layer in a quilt and its thickness really determines how raised the quilting pattern will be. There are now many different types of wadding available but polyester is the most common. Setsuko Obi, like many quilters, prefers the 2oz weight of polyester, which is the thinnest, but still gives an extra dimension to the quilt. Deirdre Amsden prefers to match the type of wadding to the fabrics used in the patchwork top. For example, she uses a manufactured wool wadding with wool/cotton fabric (Viyella) and a cotton one for patchwork made from cotton fabrics. The cotton wadding is the filling most frequently found in older quilts and needs to be used with the fluffy side up. To prevent the loose fibres working through to the top surface, Deirdre places a piece of muslin between these two layers before tacking. The cotton wadding needs to be more closely quilted and is heavier than the polyester, which is easier to wash.

The choice of wadding is determined by the type of quilt you are making and its use. I prefer the extra weight and body that the wool or cotton wadding gives. It makes a quilt feel more substantial, whether it is used as a hanging or on a bed. For something in everyday use perhaps a polyester wadding is more suitable. Old blankets were a popular filling when warmth and economy were the prime motivations for quiltmaking, but the extra thickness made quilting more difficult. Cotton domett, which is similar to felt, is another alternative, but requires dry cleaning.

It is becoming more commonplace to buy wadding in bed sizes which avoids having to join lengths together. If you do need to do this, butt the wadding together and join with a loose overcast stitch rather than overlapping it which will make a noticeable ridge.

Thread Special quilting thread can now be purchased, but there are alternatives that serve the purpose equally well. Whatever your choice, make sure it is strong enough

to stitch and hold the layers together. A pure cotton No 40 or silk thread for silk fabrics is available. For a slightly heavier stitch try a cotton perlé. Running the thread through beeswax does make it easier to work with and – as with all hand-sewing – it helps to knot the end that you cut. Tacking cotton is also required.

Templates Templates are needed to draw around to mark the quilting design on the top fabric. A metre or yard rule is useful for marking straight lines; masking tape provides a quick temporary guide.

The templates can be cut from the same material as is used for patchwork. Heavy brown paper was once commonly used, and this is handy for making shapes from folded paper. Plastic templates can be purchased but the choice is limited and eventually it is better to make your own. The shape represents the pattern outline: inside details are filled in by hand.

TRADITIONAL TEMPLATES

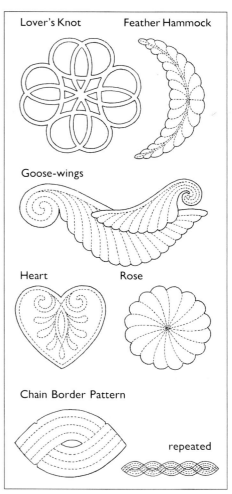

Marking quilting patterns

Experienced traditional quilters often marked out the pattern as the work progressed in the frame unless they had had the quilt top marked by a professional like Mary Fairless. They used a large blunt-ended needle pressed against the template which made an indented line to follow, as described by Jane Snaith. When using a hoop, the quilting design needs to be marked out completely before the layers are tacked together. It is best done using a Chinagraph or coloured pencil that closely matches the fabric, with the top laid over another fabric or some sheeting to stop it from slipping.

If you are making a plain quilt and using a light-coloured top fabric it is possible to draw out the design on paper and then to place this under the fabric and trace it off. Fold in half, then quarters, to mark the centre point and main divisions. Many quiltmakers start off by simply quilting around each patch, known as 'outline quilting'.

QUILTING PATTERN FOR *MAPLE LEAF* QUILT

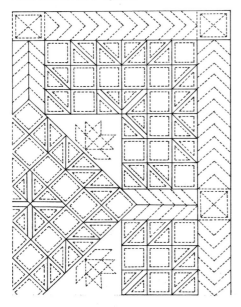

Preparing the layers

The three layers (or four if you add muslin) need to be thoroughly tacked together before being put into the hoop.

Cut the wadding and backing slightly larger than the required size so that it can be trimmed after quilting. If you are taking the top over the back or the back over the top for self-bound edges, include this in the calculation (see page 155).

Unless the quilt is small, it is easiest to work on the floor at this stage. To assemble the layers together first mark the centre points around the edges on all three layers. Take the backing fabric and place right side down, then put the wadding on top so that the centre points of both layers align. Place the top right side up on the wadding, again matching centre points around edges. Gently smooth out any wrinkles. Alternatively tack the layers together using a frame; see Gill Horn's method on pages 109–10.

Tacking the layers together

Start tacking from the centre outwards. If it is difficult to reach the centre, gently roll up one side and work in two halves. To avoid having a bunch of knots in the centre, take a long length of tacking cotton and using only half tack diagonally to one corner. Return and tack to the other. Continue in this way and tack to all corners, then to equally spaced points in between. Return to the centre and tack a series of concentric lines about 10cm/4in apart until you reach the outside edge.

Using a hoop

Always start quilting at the centre of the work, then gradually move outwards. Begin by placing the work right side up over the inside hoop. Slightly loosen the outer hoop and place this over the work and inner hoop. Gently ease out any unevenness so that the work is flat, then tighten the outer hoop so that the work is held securely but with enough give to enable several stitches to be taken at once. Check the back to make sure it is smooth. As each area is quilted, loosen the hoop and move to a

new area, gradually working outwards until the quilting is complete. Avoid leaving work in the hoop if it is not being quilted, as there is a risk of permanently marking the fabric. Deirdre Amsden covers the outer hoop with a bandage of fabric, which not only helps to get a better grip but reduces the risk of marking the quilt top.

The quilting stitch

The quilting pattern is made with a small evenly spaced running stitch worked on the top side. The size depends on the thickness of wadding. Aim to sew in continuous lines and when you have reached the boundary of the hoop let the thread hang so that it is ready to be picked up once the hoop is moved to a new area. The stitches should be the same length as the spaces between, and even back and front. All this comes with practice, so do not worry if it is not right the first time! The hands work in unison, so rest the hoop on the edge of a table for support.

POSITION OF HANDS

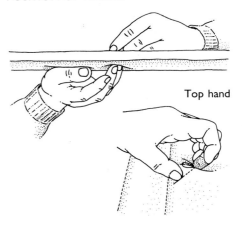

Top hand

USING A HOOP

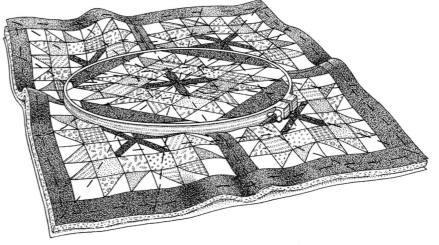

To begin cut a length of thread about 40cm/16in and knot the cut end. From the top insert the needle close to the marked line and pull the thread through so that the knot becomes trapped in the wadding. Bring the needle back up to the line and begin quilting. Do this by having the sewing hand on top with a thimble on the second finger which guides the needle down through the layers. The thumb is naturally placed just ahead of the stitching so that it is pressing down the fabric as the needle comes to the top. The other hand is placed under the work so that the fingers feel the needle going through the layers and guide it back up again. There are several ways of finishing a line of stitching. One is to make a knot close to the last stitch and to take the thread through to the back so that the knot is again trapped in the wadding, then to trim the end. Alternatively, make a small backstitch, splitting the previous stitch, and lose the end in the wadding.

Quilting edges and corners

To complete the quilting around the edges and in the corners, tack lengths of cotton fabric about 20cm/8in wide to the sides. Make sure they overlap at the corners. This extends the area of the work and enables it to be quilted in the hoop as before.

QUILTING A CORNER

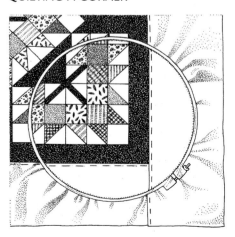

Above *Deirdre Amsden quilting* Checkerboard Squares *with a hoop.*

MACHINE-QUILTING

Machine-quilting produces a harder line and has a mechanical appearance. This effect can be reduced if you use transparent thread (as seen with Jo Budd's latest work). Machine quilting is more suitable for straight lines and simple patterns that do not require the work to be constantly turned. Mary Fogg uses an industrial machine that does make the stitching easier, but until recently Pauline Burbidge quilted all her work on a domestic machine, sinking the stitching into the seam so that it was hidden. The quality of machine quilting does make it more suitable for contemporary than for traditional designs. I have frequently used machine quilting and found it easier to quilt the blocks individually before joining them into one piece, as handling a large bulky quilt seems one of the main problems. For machine quilting it is also easier to use a flatter wadding. I used cotton domett, and although it did not give a raised pattern, the quilt felt more substantial.

The process is made much easier if you work at a table large enough to support the weight of the complete quilt during stitching. It is still necessary to prepare the three layers before machine quilting. Unless the pattern consists of simple straight lines – when a quilting foot can be used – it is easier if the quilting pattern is marked on the top before assembling the layers together.

Tacking the layers together

With small quilts the layers can be tacked in the same way as for hand-quilting. Keep the tacking stitches fairly small so that they will not get tangled with the presser foot. For large quilts, double tack. (That is, first tack the backing and wadding together, then add the top and tack together.)

The three layers can be pinned thoroughly together, thus avoiding any tacking work. Keep the pins parallel to the marked lines with the points placed towards the presser foot, which makes it easier to remove them as the work progresses.

Using a quilting foot

For machine-quilting use a longer stitch and loosen the tension. With a quilting foot you only need mark the centre line. Decide on the width between lines and adjust the bar accordingly. Start at the top centre, aligning the bar edge with the marked line. Stitch the first line of stitches, then return to the top and this time align the bar with the line of stitches. Continue in this way – aligning the bar against the previous stitched line – until the first half is complete. Then work on the other side.

For a pattern of squares, work at right angles to these lines. If all the ends are at the edge of the work they will be trimmed and hidden under the finished edge. If there are ends elsewhere, pull them through to the back and finish off by hand. Avoid beginning and ending rows with backstitches, as this looks untidy on the front and back.

USING A QUILTING FOOT

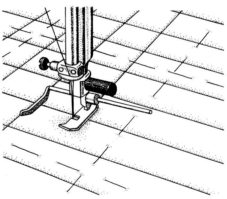

Sink stitching is only visible on the underside, as the stitches are hidden in the seam at the top. Pin or tack the layers together. To reduce the bulk when machine-quilting, roll up the quilt on either side so that only the area you are stitching is exposed. Guide the work flat through the machine, but at the same time open up the seam so that the line of stitches can sink down and be hidden. Aim to work always in the same direction to keep the layers from pulling away from each other. Again take all the ends to the back and finish by hand. If the quilt is very large, try working in quarters, or in half, then join the sections together later.

Finishing the edges

Once the quilting is complete, the edges can be finished. The simplest method is to turn both the raw edges in and to trim the wadding back to just inside. For a quilt that

Above Detail of machine quilting. *Shipshape. Pauline Burbidge.*
Opposite page Details of the edges of quilts made by *Setsuko Obi.*

EDGES FOLDED IN

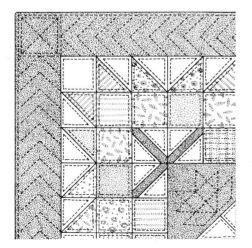

SELF-BOUND EDGE

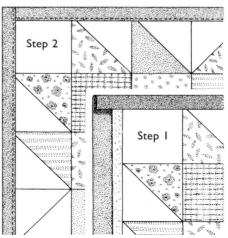

Step 2

Step 1

has been hand-stitched, finish with one or two lines of running stitch. This can also be done on machine quilts, as hand-stitching is easier to work close to the edge.

The edges can be self-bound by cutting the backing fabric slightly larger than the top and bringing it over to the front. Remember to leave enough wadding to fill the edges.

STORING QUILTS

Quilts are best rolled up for storage. Cover several cardboard tubes with acid-free tissue paper and roll the quilt around the tubes with the top side outermost.

Avoid ironing quilts, as this flattens the quilting. To remove any creases, use an electric steam clothes brush. □

USEFUL ADDRESSES

STOCKISTS (mail order)
Dyeing and stencilling on cloth

CANDLE MAKERS SUPPLIES
28 Blythe Road, London W14 0HA
(Materials for batik, fabric dyes and
painting on fabric etc.)

DURHAM CHEMICALS DISTRIBUTORS
LTD
55–7 Glengall Road, London SE15
(Helizarin dyes, pigment/binder system,
Procion dyes, Bricoprint Opaque white)

X-FILM
PO Box 37, 34 Bilton Way
Luton LU1 1UU
(Stencil film which is self-adhesive and re-
usable)

Fabric and equipment

WHALEYS (BRADFORD) LTD
Harris Court, Great Horton
Bradford, West Yorkshire BD7 4EQ
(Wide range of natural fibres, many
prepared for dyeing and printing)

GEORGE WEIL & SONS LTD
63–5 Riding House Street
London W1P 7PP
(Cottons and silks)

STRAWBERRY FAYRE
Chagford, Devon TQ13 8EN
(Wide colour range of plain and printed
fabrics in pure cotton, plus quilting
supplies and quilt-size wadding)

THE PATCHWORK DOG AND THE
CALICO CAT
21 Chalk Farm Road, London NW1
(Quiltmaking supplies including fabric,
antique quilts and books)

Associations

NATIONAL PATCHWORK
ASSOCIATION
PO Box 300
Hethersett, Norwich, Norfolk NR9 3DB
(Organises The National Patchwork
Championships. Open to anyone
interested in quiltmaking.)

THE QUILTER'S GUILD
OP66, Dean Clough, Halifax HX3 5AX
(Open to anyone who works in
patchwork, appliqué and quilting or who
has a specialized interest in quilts).

QUILT ART
Christine Mitchell
9 Old South Close, Hatch End, Pinner
Middlesex HA5 4TW
(Membership by selection, for quiltmakers
working to extend the boundaries of the
medium).

Publications

TRADITIONAL BRITISH QUILTS
Dorothy Osler,
Batsford

THE QUILTS OF THE BRITISH ISLES
Janet Rae
Constable

INTERNATIONAL
CANADIAN QUILTERS ASSOCIATION
PO Box CP22010
Heron Gate Postal Outlet
Ottawa
Ontario K1V OC2
Canada

AUSTRALIAN QUILTERS GUILD INC
PO 654
Neutral Bay Junction
NSW 2089
Australia

PACIFIC QUILTS (Magazine)
35 Target Road
Glenfield
Auckland 10
New Zealand

THE FINE ART OF QUILTING
Vicki Barker and Tessa Bird
Studio Vista

THE COMPLETE BOOK OF QUILTMAKING
Michele Walker
Windward/Frances Lincoln

Museum
THE EARLE HILL HEAD FARM MUSEUM
Wooler
Northumberland NE17 6RH
0668 81243
(check opening times before visiting)

*Jenny and Alec Hutchinson
dispatching fabrics from Strawberry Fayre.
(mail order only)*

INDEX

Opposite page *Detail of* Duo. *Gill Horn. (See page 106)*

ACKNOWLEDGMENTS

PHOTOGRAPHER
SANDRA LOUSADA
Assisted by
CLARE PAXTON

EDITOR
PENNY DAVID

ART EDITOR
MICHELE WALKER

ILLUSTRATOR
JANE CRADOCK-WATSON

Typesetter
TEXTYPE TYPESETTERS
CAMBRIDGE

**Printed and bound
in Italy by**
NEW INTERLITHO
S.p.a., Milan

The author would like to thank the following for their contribution towards the making of this book:

Sandra Lousada, without whose special qualities as a photographer and friend this book would not be as it is. Clare Paxton for her caring assistance and Sandra's agent, Susan Griggs, for continual encouragement and support throughout the project.

Penny David for her thoughtful editorial contribution and expert guidance in shaping the book and helping to translate my ideas into print. Jane Cradock-Watson for her attractive illustrations.

Fiona MacIntyre at Ebury Press for her initial support and perserverance in keeping the book to schedule, and Brenda Glover for overseeing the production.

Ron Simpson and Jen Jones for the generous loan of quilts from their collections; Mrs Armstrong of The Earle Hill Head Farm Museum; Marion Oates of The Alnwick Tourist Board; Christine Stevens of The Welsh Folk Museum, St Fagans; Rosemary Allan of Beamish Museum; Textile Department, Trent Polytechnic, Nottingham; Benjamin Britten High School, Lowestoft; Lancashire County Library; The Quilters' Guild (Tape archives); Judy Downing; Shirley Webster; Ann Cannings and Maxine Pugh for typing my original taped interviews.

Last, but not least, a special thank you to Mrs Snaith, Miss Fairless, Mrs Lewis, Jean Sheers, Eiluned Edwards, Deirdre Amsden, Janet Bolton, Lucinda Gane, Liz Bruce, Pauline Burbidge, Linda Straw, Lucy Goffin, Gillian Horn, Jo Budd, Setsuko Obi and Mary Fogg.

Above Dreamcoat *Man's waistcoat. 1989. Lucy Goffin.*
Jacket Crazyquilt *(detail). English. 1894–1920. 163×188 cm/64×74 in.*